BRION GYSIN

DABA

PERMUTATIONS

New York

I AM THAT I AM
I AM THAT I
AM I AM THAT
I AM
I AM
THAT I AM

I AM THAT I AM
I AM THAT AM I
AM I THAT
I AM
AM I I THAT AM
I THAT I AM AM

AM THAT I AM I
THAT I AM I AM
THAT AM I I AM
THAT I AM AM I
THAT I I AM AM
THAT AM I AM I
I THAT AM AM I
I I THAT AM AM
I AM I AM THAT
I AM AM I THAT
AM I THAT I AM

AM I AM I THAT
AM I AM I THAT
AM I AM I THAT
AM I AM I THAT
AM I AM I THAT
AM I THAT
AM I THAT
AM I
AM I
AM I
AM I
AM I

I AM THAT I AM
I AM THAT I
AM I
AM THAT
I AM
I AM THAT I AM
I AM THAT I AM

<table>
<tr><td>I</td><td>AM</td><td>THAT</td><td>I</td><td>AM</td><td></td></tr>
<tr><td>I</td><td>AM</td><td>THAT</td><td>I</td><td></td><td></td></tr>
<tr><td>AM</td><td>I</td><td></td><td>AM</td><td>THAT</td><td></td></tr>
<tr><td>I</td><td>AM</td><td></td><td>I</td><td>AM</td><td></td></tr>
<tr><td>THAT</td><td>I</td><td>AM</td><td></td><td></td><td></td></tr>
</table>

<table>
<tr><td>I</td><td>AM</td><td>THAT</td><td>I</td><td>AM</td><td></td></tr>
<tr><td>I</td><td>AM</td><td>THAT</td><td>AM</td><td>I</td><td></td></tr>
<tr><td>AM</td><td>I</td><td>THAT</td><td></td><td>I</td><td>AM?</td></tr>
</table>

<table>
<tr><td>AM</td><td>I</td><td>I</td><td>THAT</td><td>AM?</td><td></td></tr>
<tr><td>I</td><td>THAT</td><td>I</td><td>AM</td><td>AM</td><td></td></tr>
<tr><td>AM</td><td>THAT</td><td>I</td><td>AM</td><td>I</td><td></td></tr>
<tr><td>THAT</td><td>I</td><td>AM</td><td>I</td><td>AM</td><td></td></tr>
<tr><td>THAT</td><td>AM</td><td>I</td><td>I</td><td>AM</td><td></td></tr>
<tr><td>THAT</td><td>I</td><td>AM.</td><td></td><td>AM</td><td>I?</td></tr>
<tr><td>THAT</td><td>I</td><td>I</td><td>AM</td><td>AM</td><td></td></tr>
<tr><td>THAT</td><td>AM</td><td>I</td><td></td><td>AM</td><td>I</td></tr>
<tr><td>I</td><td>THAT</td><td>AM</td><td>AM</td><td>I</td><td></td></tr>
<tr><td>I</td><td>I</td><td>THAT</td><td>AM</td><td>AM</td><td></td></tr>
<tr><td>I</td><td>AM</td><td>I</td><td>AM</td><td>THAT</td><td></td></tr>
<tr><td>I</td><td>AM,</td><td></td><td>AM</td><td>I,</td><td>—THAT?</td></tr>
<tr><td>AM</td><td>I</td><td>THAT</td><td>I</td><td>AM?</td><td></td></tr>
</table>

<table>
<tr><td>I</td><td>AM</td><td>THAT</td><td>I</td><td>AM</td><td></td></tr>
<tr><td>I</td><td>AM</td><td>I</td><td>THAT</td><td>AM</td><td></td></tr>
<tr><td>I</td><td>AM</td><td>AM</td><td>I</td><td></td><td>THAT</td></tr>
<tr><td>I</td><td>AM</td><td>THAT</td><td>AM</td><td>I</td><td></td></tr>
<tr><td>I</td><td>AM</td><td>I</td><td>AM</td><td>THAT</td><td></td></tr>
<tr><td>I</td><td>AM</td><td>AM</td><td>THAT</td><td></td><td>I</td></tr>
</table>

<table>
<tr><td>AM</td><td>THAT</td><td>I</td><td>AM</td><td></td><td>I</td></tr>
<tr><td>AM</td><td>THAT</td><td></td><td>AM</td><td>I</td><td>I</td></tr>
<tr><td>AM</td><td>THAT</td><td>I</td><td>I</td><td>AM</td><td></td></tr>
<tr><td>AM</td><td>THAT</td><td>I</td><td></td><td>I</td><td>AM</td></tr>
<tr><td>AM</td><td>THAT</td><td></td><td>AM</td><td>I</td><td>I</td></tr>
<tr><td>AM</td><td>THAT</td><td></td><td>I</td><td>AM</td><td>I</td></tr>
</table>

A handwritten note reads: "timing by Douglas Cleverdon who produced the programme *Permutated Poems of Brion Gysin*, Aug. 15, 1961."

THAT I AM I AM
THAT I I AM AM
THAT I AM I AM
THAT I AM AM I
THAT I I AM AM
THAT I AM AM I

I AM I AM THAT
I AM AM I THAT
I AM THAT AM I
I AM THAT I AM
I AM AM THAT I
I AM I AM THAT

AM I I THAT AM
AM I THAT AM I
AM I AM I THAT
AM I I AM THAT
AM I THAT I AM
AM I AM THAT I

THAT AM I AM I
THAT AM AM I I
THAT AM I I AM
THAT AM I I AM
THAT AM AM I I
THAT AM I AM I

AM AM I THAT I
AM AM THAT I I
AM AM I I THAT
AM AM I I THAT
AM AM THAT I I
AM AM I THAT I

I I AM THAT AM
I I THAT AM AM
I I AM THAT AM
I I AM THAT AM
I I THAT AM AM
I I AM AM THAT

I AM THAT I AM .
I AM THAT I . AM
I AM THAT . I AM
I AM . THAT I AM
I . AM THAT I AM

AM I THAT AM I .
AM I THAT AM . I
AM I THAT . AM I
AM I . THAT AM I
AM . I THAT AM I

I AM THAT AM I .
I AM THAT AM . I
I AM THAT . AM I
I AM . THAT AM I
I . AM THAT AM I

AM I THAT I AM .
AM I THAT I . AM
AM I THAT . I AM
AM I . THAT I AM
AM . I THAT I AM

I THAT I AM AM .
I THAT AM AM . I .
I THAT AM . AM I
I THAT AM AM I
I . THAT AM AM I

AM I I THAT AM .
AM I I THAT . AM
AM I I . THAT AM
AM I . I THAT AM
AM . I I THAT AM

THAT I AM I AM .
THAT I AM I . AM
THAT I AM . I AM
THAT I . AM I AM
THAT . I AM I AM

AM I AM I THAT .
AM I AM I . THAT
AM I AM . I THAT
AM I . AM I THAT
AM . I AM I THAT

I I THAT AM AM .
I I THAT AM . AM
I I THAT . AM AM
I I . THAT AM AM
I . I THAT AM AM

THAT AM I I AM .
THAT AM I I . AM
THAT AM I . I AM
THAT AM . I I AM
THAT . AM I I AM

AM I AM THAT AM .
AM I AM THAT . I
AM I AM . THAT I
AM I . AM THAT I
AM . I AM THAT I

I AM I AM THAT .
I AM I AM . THAT
I AM I . AM THAT
I AM . I AM THAT
I . AM I AM THAT

THAT I AM AM I .
THAT I AM AM . I
THAT I AM . AM I
THAT I . AM AM I
THAT . I AM AM I

AM I AM THAT I .
AM I AM THAT . I
AM I AM . THAT I
AM I . AM THAT I
AM . I AM THAT I

I AM AM I THAT .
I AM AM I . THAT
I AM AM . I THAT
I AM . AM I THAT
I . AM AM I THAT

THAT I I AM AM .
THAT I I AM . AM
THAT I I . AM AM
THAT I . I AM AM
THAT . I I AM AM

AM THAT I AM I .
AM THAT I AM . I
AM THAT I . AM I
AM THAT . I AM I
AM . THAT I AM I

I AM I THAT AM .
I AM I THAT . AM
I AM I . THAT AM
I AM . I THAT AM
I . AM I THAT AM

THAT AM I AM I .
THAT AM I AM . I
THAT AM I . AM I
THAT AM . I AM I
THAT . AM I AM A

AM THAT I I AM .
AM THAT I I . AM
AM THAT I . I AM
AM THAT . I I AM
AM . THAT I I AM

I AM I THAT AM .
I AM I THAT . AM
I AM I . THAT AM
I AM . I THAT AM
I . AM I THAT AM

THAT AM AM I I .
THAT AM AM I . I
THAT AM AM . I I
THAT AM . AM I I
THAT . AM AM I I

AM THAT AM I I .
AM THAT AM I . I
AM THAT AM . I I
AM THAT . AM I I
AM . THAT AM I I

I AM AM THAT I .
I AM AM THAT . I
I AM AM . THAT I
I AM . AM THAT I
I . AM AM THAT I

AM		AM		I		I		THAT	.
AM		AM		I		I	.	THAT	
AM		AM		I	.	I		THAT	
AM		AM	.	I		I		THAT	
AM	.	AM		I		I		THAT	
I		THAT		AM		I		AM	.
I		THAT		AM		I	.	AM	
I		THAT		AM	.	I		AM	
I		THAT	.	AM		I		AM	
I	.	THAT		AM		I		AM	
I		THAT		AM		AM		I	.
I		AM		I		AM	.	AM	.
I		AM		I	.	AM		AM	
I		AM	.	I		AM		AM	
I	.	AM		I		AM		AM	
AM		AM		THAT		I		I	.
AM		AM		THAT		I	.	I	
AM		AM		THAT	.	I		I	
AM		AM	.	THAT		I		I	
AM	.	AM		THAT		I		I	
I		I		AM		AM		THAT	.
I		I		AM		AM	.	THAT	
I		I		AM	.	AM		THAT	
I		I	.	AM		AM		THAT	
I	.	I		AM		AM		THAT	
I		I		AM		THAT		AM	
I		I		AM		THAT		AM	
I		I		AM		THAT		AM	
I		I		AM		THAT		AM	
I		I		AM		THAT		AM	

I	AM	THAT	I	AM	
I	AM	I	THAT	AM	
I	AM	AM	I		THAT
I	AM	THAT	AM	I	
I	AM	I	AM	THAT	
I	AM	AM	THAT		I

AM	THAT	I	AM		I
AM	THAT		AM	I	I
AM	THAT	I	I	AM	
AM	THAT	I		I	AM
AM	THAT		AM	I	I
AM	THAT		I	AM	I

THAT I AM I AM
THAT I I AM AM
THAT I AM I AM
THAT I AM AM I
THAT I I AM AM
THAT I AM AM I

I AM I AM THAT
I AM AM I THAT
I AM THAT AM I
I AM THAT I AM
I AM AM THAT I
I AM I AM THAT

AM I I THAT AM
AM I THAT AM I
AM I AM I THAT
AM I I AM THAT
AM I THAT I AM
AM I AM THAT I

THAT AM I AM I
THAT AM AM I I
THAT AM I I AM
THAT AM I I AM
THAT AM AM I I
THAT AM I AM I

AM AM I THAT I
AM AM THAT I I
AM AM I I THAT
AM AM I I THAT
AM AM THAT I I
AM AM I THAT I

I I AM THAT AM
I I THAT AM AM
I I AM THAT AM
I I AM THAT AM
I I THAT AM AM
I I AM AM THAT

"The whole idea of the permutations came to me visually on seeing the so-called, Divine Tautology, in print. It looked wrong, to me, non-symmetrical. The biggest word, That, belonged in the middle but all I had to do was switch the last two words and It asked a question: 'I Am That, Am I?' The rest followed."

B.G.

I AM THAT I AM
AM I THAT I AM
I THAT AM I AM
THAT I AM I AM
AM THAT I I AM
THAT AM I I AM
I AM I THAT AM
AM I I THAT AM
I I AM THAT AM
I I AM THAT AM
AM I I THAT AM
I AM I THAT AM
I THAT I AM AM
THAT I I AM AM
I I THAT AM AM
I I THAT AM AM
THAT I I AM AM
I THAT I AM AM
AM THAT I I AM
THAT AM I I AM
AM I THAT I AM
I AM THAT I AM
THAT I AM I AM
I THAT AM I AM
I AM THAT AM I
AM I THAT AM I
I THAT AM AM I
THAT I AM AM I
AM THAT I AM I
THAT AM I AM I

I AM AM THAT I
AM I AM THAT I
I AM AM THAT I
AM I AM THAT I
AM AM I THAT I
AM AM I THAT I
I THAT AM AM I
THAT I AM AM I
I AM THAT AM I
AM I THAT AM I
THAT AM I AM I
AM THAT I AM I
AM THAT AM I I
THAT AM AM I I
AM AM THAT I I
AM AM THAT I I
THAT AM AM I I
AM THAT AM I I
I AM I AM THAT
AM I I AM THAT
I I AM AM THAT
I I AM AM THAT
AM I I AM THAT
I AM I AM THAT
I AM AM I THAT
AM I AM I THAT
I AM AM I THAT
AM I AM I THAT
AM AM I I THAT
AM AM I I THAT

I I AM AM THAT
I I AM AM THAT
I AM I AM THAT
AM I I AM THAT
I AM I AM THAT
AM I I AM THAT
AM I AM I THAT
I AM AM I THAT
AM AM I I THAT
AM AM I I THAT
I AM AM I THAT
AM I AM I THAT
I THAT I AM AM
THAT I I AM AM
I I THAT AM AM
I I THAT AM AM
THAT I I AM AM
I THAT I AM AM
I THAT AM I AM
THAT I AM I AM
I AM THAT I AM
AM I THAT I AM
THAT AM I I AM
AM THAT I I AM
I I AM THAT AM
I I AM THAT AM
I AM I THAT AM
AM I I THAT AM
I AM I THAT AM
AM I I THAT AM
THAT I AM I AM
I THAT AM I AM
THAT AM I I AM
AM THAT I I AM
I AM THAT I AM
AM I THAT I AM
AM THAT I AM I
THAT AM I AM I

AM I THAT AM I
I AM THAT AM I
THAT I AM AM I
I THAT AM AM I
AM THAT AM I I
THAT AM AM I I
AM AM THAT I I
AM AM THAT I I
THAT AM AM I I
AM THAT AM I I
AM I AM THAT I
I AM AM THAT I
AM AM I THAT I
AM AM I THAT I
I AM AM THAT I
AM I AM THAT I
THAT I AM AM I
I THAT AM AM I
THAT AM I AM I
AM THAT I AM I
I AM THAT AM I
AM I THAT AM I
AM I AM THAT I
AM AM I THAT I
AM I THAT AM I
AM THAT I AM I
AM AM THAT I I
AM THAT AM I I
AM I AM I THAT
AM AM I I THAT
AM I I AM THAT
AM I I AM THAT
AM AM I I THAT
AM I AM I THAT
AM I THAT I AM
AM THAT I I AM
AM I I THAT AM
AM I I THAT AM

AM THAT I I AM
AM I THAT I AM
AM AM THAT I I
AM THAT AM I I
AM AM I THAT I
AM I AM THAT I
AM THAT I AM I
AM I THAT AM I
I I AM THAT AM
I AM I THAT AM
I I THAT AM AM
I THAT I AM AM
I AM THAT I AM
I THAT AM I AM
I I AM AM THAT
I AM I AM THAT
I I AM AM THAT
I AM I AM THAT
I AM AM I THAT
I AM AM I THAT
I I THAT AM AM
I THAT I AM AM
I I AM THAT AM
I AM I THAT AM
I THAT AM I AM
I AM THAT I AM
I AM THAT AM I
I THAT AM AM I
I AM AM THAT I
I AM AM THAT I
I THAT AM AM I
I AM THAT AM I
THAT I AM I AM
THAT AM I I AM
THAT I I AM AM
THAT I I AM AM
THAT AM I I AM
THAT I AM I AM

THAT I AM AM I
THAT AM I AM I
THAT I AM AM I
THAT AM I AM I
THAT AM AM I I
THAT AM AM I I
THAT I I AM AM
THAT I I AM AM
THAT I AM I AM
THAT AM I I AM
THAT I AM I AM
THAT AM I I AM
THAT AM I AM I
THAT I AM AM I
THAT AM AM I I
THAT AM AM I I
THAT I AM AM I
THAT AM I AM I
AM I THAT I AM
AM THAT I I AM
AM I I THAT AM
AM I I THAT AM
AM THAT I I AM
AM I THAT I AM
AM I THAT AM I
AM THAT I AM I
AM I AM THAT I
AM AM I THAT I
AM THAT AM I I
AM AM THAT I I
AM I I AM THAT
AM I I AM THAT
AM I AM I THAT
AM AM I I THAT
AM I AM I THAT
AM AM I I THAT
AM THAT I AM I
AM I THAT AM I

AM THAT AM I I
AM AM THAT I I
AM I AM THAT I
AM AM I THAT I
I AM THAT I AM
I THAT AM I AM
I AM I THAT AM
I I AM THAT AM
I THAT I AM AM
I I THAT AM AM
I AM THAT AM I
I THAT AM AM I
I AM AM THAT I
I AM AM THAT I
I THAT AM AM I
I AM THAT AM I
I AM I AM THAT
I I AM AM THAT
I AM AM I THAT
I AM AM I THAT
I I AM AM THAT
I AM I AM THAT
I THAT I AM AM
I I THAT AM AM
I THAT AM I AM
I AM THAT I AM
I I AM THAT AM
I AM I THAT AM
I AM I AM THAT
I AM AM I THAT
I AM I THAT AM
I AM THAT I AM
I AM AM THAT I
I AM THAT AM I
THAT AM I AM I
THAT AM AM I I
THAT AM I I AM
THAT AM I I AM

THAT AM AM I I
THAT AM I AM I
AM AM I THAT I
AM AM THAT I I
AM AM I I THAT
AM AM I I THAT
AM AM THAT I I
AM AM I THAT I
I AM AM THAT I
I AM THAT AM I
I AM AM I THAT
I AM I AM THAT
I AM THAT I AM
I AM I THAT AM
AM I I AM THAT
AM I AM I THAT
AM I I THAT AM
AM I THAT I AM
AM I AM THAT I
AM I THAT AM I
THAT I I AM AM
THAT I AM I AM
THAT I I AM AM
THAT I AM I AM
THAT I AM AM I
THAT I AM AM I
AM I I THAT AM
AM I THAT I AM
AM I I AM THAT
AM I AM I THAT
AM I THAT AM I
AM I AM THAT I
I I AM THAT AM
I I THAT AM AM
I I AM AM THAT
I I AM AM THAT
I I THAT AM AM
I I AM THAT AM

AM THAT I AM I
AM THAT AM I I
AM THAT I I AM
AM THAT I I AM
AM THAT AM I I
AM THAT I AM I
I THAT I AM AM
I THAT AM I AM
I THAT I AM AM
I THAT AM I AM
I THAT AM AM I
I THAT AM AM I
AM THAT I I AM
AM THAT I I AM
AM THAT I AM I
AM THAT AM I I
AM THAT I AM I
AM THAT AM I I
I THAT AM I AM
I THAT I AM AM
I THAT AM AM I
I THAT AM AM I
I THAT I AM AM
I THAT AM I AM
AM AM I THAT I
AM AM THAT I I
AM AM I I THAT
AM AM I I THAT
AM AM THAT I I
AM AM I THAT I
I AM I THAT AM
I AM THAT I AM
I AM I AM THAT
I AM AM I THAT
I AM THAT AM I
I AM AM THAT I
THAT AM I I AM
THAT AM I I AM
THAT AM I AM I

THAT AM AM I I
THAT AM I AM I
THAT AM AM I I
I AM THAT I AM
I AM I THAT AM
I AM THAT AM I
I AM AM THAT I
I AM I AM THAT
I AM AM I THAT
AM I AM THAT I
AM I THAT AM I
AM I AM I THAT
AM I I AM THAT
AM I THAT I AM
AM I I THAT AM
I I AM THAT AM
I I THAT AM AM
I I AM AM THAT
I I AM AM THAT
I I THAT AM AM
I I AM THAT AM
THAT I AM I AM
THAT I I AM AM
THAT I AM AM I
THAT I AM AM I
THAT I I AM AM
THAT I AM I AM
AM I THAT I AM
AM I I THAT AM
AM I THAT AM I
AM I AM THAT I
AM I I AM THAT
AM I AM I THAT
THAT I AM I AM
THAT I AM AM I
AM I AM I THAT
AM I AM THAT I
I I AM AM THAT
I I AM THAT AM

I THAT AM I AM
I THAT AM AM I
AM THAT AM I I
AM THAT AM I I
I THAT AM AM I
I THAT AM I AM
I AM AM I THAT
I AM AM THAT I
THAT AM AM I I
THAT AM AM I I
I AM AM THAT I
I AM AM I THAT
I I AM AM THAT
I I AM THAT AM
THAT I AM AM I
THAT I AM I AM
AM I AM THAT I
AM I AM I THAT
THAT AM I I AM
THAT AM I AM I
AM AM I I THAT
AM AM I THAT I
I AM I AM THAT
I AM I THAT AM
AM THAT I I AM
AM THAT I AM I
AM THAT I I AM
AM THAT I AM I
I THAT I AM AM
I THAT I AM AM
AM AM I I THAT
AM AM I THAT I
THAT AM I I AM
THAT AM I AM I
I AM I THAT AM
I AM I AM THAT
AM I I AM THAT
AM I I THAT AM
THAT I I AM AM

THAT I I AM AM
AM I I THAT AM
AM I I AM THAT
I AM THAT I AM
I AM THAT AM I
AM AM THAT I I
AM AM THAT I I
I AM THAT AM I
I AM THAT I AM
AM I THAT I AM
AM I THAT AM I
AM I THAT I AM
AM I THAT AM I
I I THAT AM AM
I I THAT AM AM
AM AM THAT I I
AM AM THAT I I
I AM THAT I AM
I AM THAT AM I
I AM THAT I AM
I AM THAT AM I
AM I THAT AM I
AM I THAT I AM
I I THAT AM AM
I I THAT AM AM
AM I THAT I AM
AM I THAT AM I
I AM AM I THAT
I AM AM THAT I
THAT AM AM I I
THAT AM AM I I
I AM AM THAT I
I AM AM I THAT
AM I AM I THAT
AM I AM THAT I
THAT I AM I AM
THAT I AM AM I
I I AM THAT AM
I I AM AM THAT

AM THAT AM I I
AM THAT AM I I
I THAT AM I AM
I THAT AM AM I
I THAT AM I AM
I THAT AM AM I
AM I AM THAT I
AM I AM I THAT
I I AM THAT AM
I I AM AM THAT
THAT I AM I AM
THAT I AM AM I
I AM I AM THAT
I AM I THAT AM
THAT AM I AM I
THAT AM I I AM
AM AM I THAT I
AM AM I I THAT
AM I I AM THAT
AM I I THAT AM
THAT I I AM AM
THAT I I AM AM
AM I I THAT AM
AM I I AM THAT
AM THAT I AM I
AM THAT I I AM
I THAT I AM AM
I THAT I AM AM
AM THAT I I AM
AM THAT I AM I
AM AM I THAT I
AM AM I I THAT
I AM I THAT AM
I AM I AM THAT
THAT AM I I AM
THAT AM I AM I
AM THAT I AM I
I THAT I AM AM
THAT AM I AM I

I AM I AM THAT
THAT I I AM AM
AM I I AM THAT
AM I THAT AM I
I I THAT AM AM
I AM THAT AM I
I AM THAT AM I
I I THAT AM AM
AM I THAT AM I
THAT I AM AM I
I I AM AM THAT
I THAT AM AM I
I THAT AM AM I
I I AM AM THAT
THAT I AM AM I
THAT I I AM AM
AM I I AM THAT
I THAT I AM AM
AM THAT I AM I
I AM I AM THAT
THAT AM I AM I
AM THAT AM I I
I THAT AM I AM
THAT AM AM I I
I AM AM I THAT
THAT I AM I AM
AM I AM I THAT
AM AM THAT I I
I AM THAT I AM
AM AM THAT I I
I AM THAT I AM
AM I THAT I AM
AM I THAT I AM
THAT AM AM I I
I AM AM I THAT
AM THAT AM I I
I THAT AM I AM
AM I AM I THAT
THAT I AM I AM

THAT AM I I AM
AM AM I I THAT
AM THAT I I AM
AM THAT I I AM
AM AM I I THAT
THAT AM I I AM
AM I AM THAT I
I I AM THAT AM
I AM AM THAT I
I AM AM THAT I
I I AM THAT AM
AM I AM THAT I
AM AM I THAT I
I AM I THAT AM
AM AM I THAT I
I AM I THAT AM
AM I I THAT AM
AM I I THAT AM
I AM AM THAT I
I AM AM THAT I
AM I AM THAT I
I I AM THAT AM
AM I AM THAT I
I I AM THAT AM
I AM I THAT AM
AM AM I THAT I
AM I I THAT AM
AM I I THAT AM
AM AM I THAT I
I AM I THAT AM
THAT I AM AM I
I I AM AM THAT
I THAT AM AM I
I THAT AM AM I
I I AM AM THAT
THAT I AM AM I
THAT AM I AM I
I AM I AM THAT
AM THAT I AM I

I THAT I AM AM
AM I I AM THAT
THAT I I AM AM
I AM THAT AM I
I AM THAT AM I
AM I THAT AM I
I I THAT AM AM
AM I THAT AM I
I I THAT AM AM
I AM I AM THAT
THAT AM I AM I
AM I I AM THAT
THAT I I AM AM
AM THAT I AM I
I THAT I AM AM
THAT I AM I AM
AM I AM I THAT
I THAT AM I AM
AM THAT AM I I
I AM AM I THAT
THAT AM AM I I
THAT AM I I AM
AM AM I I THAT
AM THAT I I AM
AM THAT I I AM
AM AM I I THAT
THAT AM I I AM
I AM THAT I AM
AM AM THAT I I
AM I THAT I AM
AM I THAT I AM
AM AM THAT I I
I AM THAT I AM
I AM AM I THAT
THAT AM AM I I
AM I AM I THAT
THAT I AM I AM
AM THAT AM I I
I THAT AM I AM

"My voice permutating the Divine Tautology as recorded by the BBC for a programme entitled: *The Permutated Poems of Brion Gysin.* Produced by Douglas Cleverdon and broadcast to the second lowest rating of audience approval registered by their poll of listeners. Still sorry to think that the lowest rating on record went to an opus by Auden and Britten. BBC dixit. On *OU* record."

B.G.

I AM THAT I AM	AM I AM THAT I	I AM I AM THAT	THAT I AM I AM	AM THAT I AM I
AM I THAT I AM	AM AM I THAT I	I AM AM I THAT	THAT I AM AM I	I THAT I AM AM
I THAT AM I AM	AM I THAT AM I	I AM I THAT AM	AM I AM I THAT	THAT AM I AM I
THAT I AM I AM	AM THAT I AM I	I AM THAT I AM	AM I AM THAT I	I AM I AM THAT
AM THAT I I AM	AM AM THAT I I	I AM AM THAT I	I I AM AM THAT	THAT I I AM AM
THAT AM I I AM	AM THAT AM I I	I AM THAT AM I	I I AM THAT AM	AM I I AM THAT
I AM I THAT AM	AM I AM I THAT	THAT AM I AM I	I THAT AM I AM	AM I THAT AM I
AM I I THAT AM	AM AM I I THAT	THAT AM AM I I	I THAT AM AM I	I I THAT AM AM
I I AM THAT AM	AM I I AM THAT	THAT AM I I AM	AM THAT AM I I	I AM THAT AM I
I I AM THAT AM	AM I I AM THAT	THAT AM I I AM	AM THAT AM I I	I AM THAT AM I
AM I I THAT AM	AM AM I I THAT	THAT AM AM I I	I THAT AM AM I	I I THAT AM AM
I AM I THAT AM	AM I AM I THAT	THAT AM I AM I	I THAT AM I AM	AM I THAT AM I
I THAT I AM AM	AM I THAT I AM	AM AM I THAT I	I AM AM I THAT	THAT I AM AM I
THAT I I AM AM	AM THAT I I AM	AM AM THAT I I	I AM AM THAT I	I I AM AM THAT
I I THAT AM AM	AM I I THAT AM	AM AM I I THAT	THAT AM AM I I	I THAT AM AM I
I I THAT AM AM	AM I I THAT AM	AM AM I I THAT	THAT AM AM I I	I THAT AM AM I
THAT I I AM AM	AM THAT I I AM	AM AM THAT I I	I AM AM THAT I	I I AM AM THAT
I THAT I AM AM	AM I THAT I AM	AM AM I THAT I	I AM AM I THAT	THAT I AM AM I
AM THAT I I AM	AM AM THAT I I	I AM AM THAT I	I I AM AM THAT	THAT I I AM AM
THAT AM I I AM	AM THAT AM I I	I AM THAT AM I	I I AM THAT AM	AM I I AM THAT
AM I THAT I AM	AM AM I THAT I	I AM AM I THAT	THAT I AM AM I	I THAT I AM AM
I AM THAT I AM	AM I AM THAT I	I AM I AM THAT	THAT I AM I AM	AM THAT I AM I
THAT I AM I AM	AM THAT I AM I	I AM THAT I AM	AM I AM THAT I	I AM I AM THAT
I THAT AM I AM	AM I THAT AM I	I AM I THAT AM	AM I AM I THAT	THAT AM I AM I
I AM THAT AM I	I I AM THAT AM	AM I I AM THAT	THAT AM I I AM	AM THAT AM I I
AM I THAT AM I	I AM I THAT AM	AM I AM I THAT	THAT AM I AM I	I THAT AM I AM
I THAT AM AM I	I I THAT AM AM	AM I I THAT AM	AM AM I I THAT	THAT AM AM I I
THAT I AM AM I	I THAT I AM AM	AM I THAT I AM	AM AM I THAT I	I AM AM I THAT
AM THAT I AM I	I AM THAT I AM	AM I AM THAT I	I AM I AM THAT	THAT I AM I AM
THAT AM I AM I	I THAT AM I AM	AM I THAT AM I	I AM I THAT AM	AM I AM I THAT
I AM AM THAT I	I I AM AM THAT	THAT I I AM AM	AM THAT I I AM	AM AM THAT I I
AM I AM THAT I	I AM I AM THAT	THAT I AM I AM	AM THAT I AM I	I AM THAT I AM
I AM AM THAT I	I I AM AM THAT	THAT I I AM AM	AM THAT I I AM	AM AM THAT I I
AM I AM THAT I	I AM I AM THAT	THAT I AM I AM	AM THAT I AM I	I AM THAT I AM
AM AM I THAT I	I AM AM I THAT	THAT I AM AM I	I THAT I AM AM	AM I THAT I AM
AM AM I THAT I	I AM AM I THAT	THAT I AM AM I	I THAT I AM AM	AM I THAT I AM
I THAT AM AM I	I I THAT AM AM	AM I I THAT AM	AM AM I I THAT	THAT AM AM I I
THAT I AM AM I	I THAT I AM AM	AM I THAT I AM	AM AM I THAT I	I AM AM I THAT
I AM THAT AM I	I I AM THAT AM	AM I I AM THAT	THAT AM I I AM	AM THAT AM I I
AM I THAT AM I	I AM I THAT AM	AM I AM I THAT	THAT AM I AM I	I THAT AM I AM
THAT AM I AM I	I THAT AM I AM	AM I THAT AM I	I AM I THAT AM	AM I AM I THAT
AM THAT I AM I	I AM THAT I AM	AM I AM THAT I	I AM I AM THAT	THAT I AM I AM
AM THAT AM I I	I AM THAT AM I	I I AM THAT AM	AM I I AM THAT	THAT AM I I AM
THAT AM AM I I	I THAT AM AM I	I I THAT AM AM	AM I I THAT AM	AM AM I I THAT
AM AM THAT I I	I AM AM THAT I	I I AM AM THAT	THAT I I AM AM	AM THAT I I AM
AM AM THAT I I	I AM AM THAT I	I I AM AM THAT	THAT I I AM AM	AM THAT I I AM
THAT AM AM I I	I THAT AM AM I	I I THAT AM AM	AM I I THAT AM	AM AM I I THAT
AM THAT AM I I	I AM THAT AM I	I I AM THAT AM	AM I I AM THAT	THAT AM I I AM
I AM I AM THAT	THAT I AM I AM	AM THAT I AM I	I AM THAT I AM	AM I AM THAT I
AM I I AM THAT	THAT AM I I AM	AM THAT AM I I	I AM THAT AM I	I I AM THAT AM
I I AM AM THAT	THAT I I AM AM	AM THAT I I AM	AM AM THAT I I	I AM AM THAT I
I I AM AM THAT	THAT I I AM AM	AM THAT I I AM	AM AM THAT I I	I AM AM THAT I
AM I I AM THAT	THAT AM I I AM	AM THAT AM I I	I AM THAT AM I	I I AM THAT AM
I AM I AM THAT	THAT I AM I AM	AM THAT I AM I	I AM THAT I AM	AM I AM THAT I
I AM AM I THAT	THAT I AM AM I	I THAT I AM AM	AM I THAT I AM	AM AM I THAT I
AM I AM I THAT	THAT AM I AM I	I THAT AM I AM	AM I THAT AM I	I AM I THAT AM
I AM AM I THAT	THAT I AM AM I	I THAT I AM AM	AM I THAT I AM	AM AM I THAT I
AM I AM I THAT	THAT AM I AM I	I THAT AM I AM	AM I THAT AM I	I AM I THAT AM
AM AM I I THAT	THAT AM AM I I	I THAT AM AM I	I I THAT AM AM	AM I I THAT AM
AM AM I I THAT	THAT AM AM I I	I THAT AM AM I	I I THAT AM AM	AM I I THAT AM

I I AM AM THAT   THAT I I AM AM   AM THAT I I AM   AM AM THAT I I   I AM AM THAT I
I I AM AM THAT   THAT I I AM AM   AM THAT I I AM   AM AM THAT I I   I AM AM THAT I
I AM I AM THAT   THAT I AM I AM   AM THAT I AM I   I AM THAT I AM   AM I AM THAT I
AM I I AM THAT   THAT AM I I AM   AM THAT AM I I   I AM THAT AM I   I I AM THAT AM
I AM I AM THAT   THAT I AM I AM   AM THAT I AM I   I AM THAT I AM   AM I AM THAT I
AM I I AM THAT   THAT AM I I AM   AM THAT AM I I   I AM THAT AM I   I I AM THAT AM
AM I AM I THAT   THAT AM I AM I   I THAT AM I AM   AM I THAT AM I   I AM I THAT AM
I AM AM I THAT   THAT I AM AM I   I THAT I AM AM   AM I THAT I AM   AM AM I THAT I
AM AM I I THAT   THAT AM AM I I   I THAT AM AM I   I I THAT AM AM   AM I I THAT AM
AM AM I I THAT   THAT AM AM I I   I THAT AM AM I   I I THAT AM AM   AM I I THAT AM
I AM AM I THAT   THAT I AM AM I   I THAT I AM AM   AM I THAT I AM   AM AM I THAT I
AM I AM I THAT   THAT AM I AM I   I THAT AM I AM   AM I THAT AM I   I AM I THAT AM
I THAT I AM AM   AM I THAT I AM   AM AM I THAT I   I AM AM I THAT   THAT I AM AM I
THAT I I AM AM   AM THAT I I AM   AM AM THAT I I   I AM AM THAT I   I I AM AM THAT
I I THAT AM AM   AM I I THAT AM   AM AM I I THAT   THAT AM AM I I   I THAT AM AM I
I I THAT AM AM   AM I I THAT AM   AM AM I I THAT   THAT AM AM I I   I THAT AM AM I
THAT I I AM AM   AM THAT I I AM   AM AM THAT I I   I AM AM THAT I   I I AM AM THAT
I THAT I AM AM   AM I THAT I AM   AM AM I THAT I   I AM AM I THAT   THAT I AM AM I
I THAT AM I AM   AM I THAT AM I   I AM I THAT AM   AM I AM I THAT   THAT AM I AM I
THAT I AM I AM   AM THAT I AM I   I AM THAT I AM   AM I AM THAT I   I AM I AM THAT
I AM THAT I AM   AM I AM THAT I   I AM I AM THAT   THAT I AM I AM   AM THAT I AM I
AM I THAT I AM   AM AM I THAT I   I AM AM I THAT   THAT I AM AM I   I THAT I AM AM
THAT AM I I AM   AM THAT AM I I   I AM THAT AM I   I I AM THAT AM   AM I I AM THAT
AM THAT I I AM   AM AM THAT I I   I AM AM THAT I   I I AM AM THAT   THAT I I AM AM
I I AM THAT AM   AM I I AM THAT   THAT AM I I AM   AM THAT AM I I   I AM THAT AM I
I I AM THAT AM   AM I I AM THAT   THAT AM I I AM   AM THAT AM I I   I AM THAT AM I
I AM I THAT AM   AM I AM I THAT   THAT AM I AM I   I THAT AM I AM   AM I THAT AM I
AM I I THAT AM   AM AM I I THAT   THAT AM AM I I   I THAT AM AM I   I I THAT AM AM
I AM I THAT AM   AM I AM I THAT   THAT AM I AM I   I THAT AM I AM   AM I THAT AM I
AM I I THAT AM   AM AM I I THAT   THAT AM AM I I   I THAT AM AM I   I I THAT AM AM
THAT I AM I AM   AM THAT I AM I   I AM THAT I AM   AM I AM THAT I   I AM I AM THAT
I THAT AM I AM   AM I THAT AM I   I AM I THAT AM   AM I AM I THAT   THAT AM I AM I
THAT AM I I AM   AM THAT AM I I   I AM THAT AM I   I I AM THAT AM   AM I I AM THAT
AM THAT I I AM   AM AM THAT I I   I AM AM THAT I   I I AM AM THAT   THAT I I AM AM
I AM THAT I AM   AM I AM THAT I   I AM I AM THAT   THAT I AM I AM   AM THAT I AM I
AM I THAT I AM   AM AM I THAT I   I AM AM I THAT   THAT I AM AM I   I THAT I AM AM
AM THAT I AM I   I AM THAT I AM   AM I AM THAT I   I AM I AM THAT   THAT I AM I AM
THAT AM I AM I   I THAT AM I AM   AM I THAT AM I   I AM I THAT AM   AM I AM I THAT
AM I THAT AM I   I AM I THAT AM   AM I AM I THAT   THAT AM I AM I   I THAT AM I AM
I AM THAT AM I   I I AM THAT AM   AM I I AM THAT   THAT AM I I AM   AM THAT AM I I
THAT I AM AM I   I THAT I AM AM   AM I THAT I AM   AM AM I THAT I   I AM AM I THAT
I THAT AM AM I   I I THAT AM AM   AM I I THAT AM   AM AM I I THAT   THAT AM AM I I
AM THAT AM I I   I AM THAT AM I   I I AM THAT AM   AM I I AM THAT   THAT AM I I AM
THAT AM AM I I   I THAT AM AM I   I I THAT AM AM   AM I I THAT AM   AM AM I I THAT
AM AM THAT I I   I AM AM THAT I   I I AM AM THAT   THAT I I AM AM   AM THAT I I AM
AM AM THAT I I   I AM AM THAT I   I I AM AM THAT   THAT I I AM AM   AM THAT I I AM
THAT AM AM I I   I THAT AM AM I   I I THAT AM AM   AM I I THAT AM   AM AM I I THAT
AM THAT AM I I   I AM THAT AM I   I I AM THAT AM   AM I I AM THAT   THAT AM I I AM
AM I AM THAT I   I AM I AM THAT   THAT I AM I AM   AM THAT I AM I   I AM THAT I AM
I AM AM THAT I   I I AM AM THAT   THAT I I AM AM   AM THAT I I AM   AM AM THAT I I
AM AM I THAT I   I AM AM I THAT   THAT I AM AM I   I THAT I AM AM   AM I THAT I AM
AM AM I THAT I   I AM AM I THAT   THAT I AM AM I   I THAT I AM AM   AM I THAT I AM
I AM AM THAT I   I I AM AM THAT   THAT I I AM AM   AM THAT I I AM   AM AM THAT I I
AM I AM THAT I   I AM I AM THAT   THAT I AM I AM   AM THAT I AM I   I AM THAT I AM
THAT I AM AM I   I THAT I AM AM   AM I THAT I AM   AM AM I THAT I   I AM AM I THAT
I THAT AM AM I   I I THAT AM AM   AM I I THAT AM   AM AM I I THAT   THAT AM AM I I
THAT AM I AM I   I THAT AM I AM   AM I THAT AM I   I AM I THAT AM   AM I AM I THAT
AM THAT I AM I   I AM THAT I AM   AM I AM THAT I   I AM I AM THAT   THAT I AM I AM
I AM THAT AM I   I I AM THAT AM   AM I I AM THAT   THAT AM I I AM   AM THAT AM I I
AM I THAT AM I   I AM I THAT AM   AM I AM I THAT   THAT AM I AM I   I THAT AM I AM

CALLING ALL RE ACTIVE AGENTS
CALLING ALL RE ACTIVE
AGENTS CALLING ALL RE
ACTIVE AGENTS CALLING ALL
ALL RE ACTIVE AGENTS

CALLING AGENTS ALL RE ACTIVE
CALLING ALL ACTIVE AGENTS RE
CALLING ALL AGENTS ACTIVE RE
CALLING ALL ACTIVE RE AGENTS
CALLING ALL AGENTS RE ACTIVE
CALLING ALL RE AGENTS ACTIVE

CALLING RE ALL ACTIVE AGENTS
CALLING RE ALL AGENTS ACTIVE
CALLING RE AGENTS ACTIVE ALL
CALLING RE AGENTS ALL ACTIVE
CALLING RE ACTIVE ALL AGENTS
CALLING RE ACTIVE AGENTS ALL

CALLING ACTIVE ALL RE AGENTS
CALLING ACTIVE RE ALL AGENTS
CALLING ACTIVE AGENTS ALL RE
CALLING ACTIVE ALL AGENTS RE
CALLING ACTIVE RE AGENTS ALL
CALLING ACTIVE AGENTS RE ALL

CALLING AGENTS ALL ACTIVE RE
CALLING AGENTS ACTIVE ALL RE
CALLING AGENTS RE ALL ACTIVE
CALLING AGENTS ALL RE ACTIVE
CALLING AGENTS ACTIVE RE ALL
CALLING AGENTS RE ACTIVE ALL

RE ALL ACTIVE AGENTS CALLING
RE ALL AGENTS CALLING ACTIVE
RE ALL CALLING AGENTS ACTIVE
RE ALL ACTIVE CALLING AGENTS
RE ALL AGENTS ACTIVE CALLING
RE ALL CALLING ACTIVE AGENTS

ALL ACTIVE RE AGENTS CALLING
ALL ACTIVE AGENTS CALLING RE
ALL ACTIVE RE CALLING AGENTS
ALL ACTIVE RE CALLING AGENTS
ALL ACTIVE AGENTS RE CALLING
ALL ACTIVE CALLING AGENTS RE

ALL AGENTS ACTIVE RE CALLING
ALL AGENTS RE ACTIVE CALLING
ALL AGENTS CALLING RE ACTIVE
ALL AGENTS ACTIVE CALLING RE
ALL AGENTS RE CALLING ACTIVE
ALL AGENTS CALLING ACTIVE RE

AGENTS ACTIVE RE CALLING ALL
ACTIVE AGENTS CALLING ALL RE
AGENTS ACTIVE ALL RE CALLING
ACTIVE AGENTS RE ALL CALLING
AGENTS ACTIVE CALLING RE ALL
ACTIVE AGENTS ALL CALLING RE

AGENTS RE ALL ACTIVE CALLING
AGENTS RE ACTIVE CALLING ALL
AGENTS RE CALLING ALL ACTIVE
AGENTS RE ALL CALLING ACTIVE
AGENTS RE ACTIVE ALL CALLING
AGENTS RE CALLING ACTIVE ALL

AGENTS CALLING ALL RE ACTIVE
AGENTS CALLING RE ALL ACTIVE
AGENTS CALLING ACTIVE ALL RE
AGENTS CALLING ALL ACTIVE RE
AGENTS CALLING RE ACTIVE ALL
AGENTS CALLING ACTIVE RE ALL

RE ACTIVE AGENTS ALL CALLING
ALL CALLING AGENTS
CALLING AGENTS ALL
RE CALLING ALL ACTIVE AGENTS
RE CALLING ACTIVE AGENTS ALL
RE CALLING AGENTS ACTIVE ALL

RE-ALL CALLING ACTIVE AGENTS . - ($ £
ALL RE-CALLING ACTIVE AGENTS - . ($ £
RE-CALLING ALL ACTIVE AGENTS . (- $ £
CALLING RE-ALL ACTIVE AGENTS (. - $ £

ALL CALLING RE-ACTIVE AGENTS - (. $ £
CALLING ALL RE-ACTIVE AGENTS (- . $ £
RE-ALL ACTIVE CALLING AGENTS . - $ (£
ALL RE-ACTIVE CALLING AGENTS - . $ (£

RE-ACTIVE ALL CALLING AGENTS . $ - (£
ACTIVE RE-ALL CALLING AGENTS $. - (£
ALL ACTIVE RE-CALLING AGENTS - $. (£
ACTIVE ALL RE-CALLING AGENTS $ - . (£

RE-CALLING ACTIVE ALL AGENTS . ($ - £
CALLING RE-ACTIVE ALL AGENTS (. $ - £
RE-ACTIVE CALLING ALL AGENTS . $ (- £
ACTIVE RE-CALLING ALL AGENTS $. (- £

CALLING ACTIVE RE-ALL AGENTS ($. - £
ACTIVE CALLING RE-ALL AGENTS $ (. - £
ALL CALLING ACTIVE RE-AGENTS - ($. £
CALLING ALL ACTIVE RE-AGENTS (- $. £

ALL ACTIVE CALLING RE-AGENTS - $ (. £
ACTIVE ALL CALLING RE-AGENTS $ - (. £
CALLING ACTIVE ALL RE-AGENTS ($ - . £
ACTIVE CALLING ALL RE-AGENTS $ (- . £

RE-ALL CALLING AGENTS ACTIVE . - (£ $
ALL RE-CALLING AGENTS ACTIVE - . (£ $
RE-CALLING ALL AGENTS ACTIVE . (- £ $
CALLING RE-ALL AGENTS ACTIVE (. - £ $

ALL CALLING RE-AGENTS ACTIVE - (. £ $
CALLING ALL RE-AGENTS ACTIVE (- . £ $
RE-ALL AGENTS CALLING ACTIVE . - £ ($
ALL RE-AGENTS CALLING ACTIVE - . £ ($

RE-AGENTS ALL CALLING ACTIVE . £ - ($
AGENTS RE-ALL CALLING ACTIVE £ . - ($
ALL AGENTS RE-CALLING ACTIVE - £ . ($
AGENTS ALL RE-CALLING ACTIVE £ - . ($

RE-CALLING AGENTS ALL ACTIVE . (£ - $
CALLING RE-AGENTS ALL ACTIVE (. £ - $
RE-AGENTS CALLING ALL ACTIVE . £ (- $
AGENTS RE-CALLING ALL ACTIVE £ . (- $

CALLING AGENTS RE-ALL ACTIVE (£ . - $
AGENTS CALLING RE-ALL ACTIVE £ (. - $
ALL CALLING AGENTS RE-ACTIVE - (£ . $
CALLING ALL AGENTS RE-ACTIVE (- £ . $

ALL AGENTS CALLING RE-ACTIVE - £ (. $
AGENTS ALL CALLING RE-ACTIVE £ - (. $
CALLING AGENTS ALL RE-ACTIVE (£ - . $
AGENTS CALLING ALL RE-ACTIVE £ (- . $

RE-ALL ACTIVE AGENTS CALLING . – $ £ (
ALL RE-ACTIVE AGENTS CALLING – . $ £ (
RE-ACTIVE ALL AGENTS CALLING . $ – £ (
ACTIVE RE-ALL AGENTS CALLING $. – £ (

ALL ACTIVE RE-AGENTS CALLING – $. £ (
ACTIVE ALL RE-AGENTS CALLING $ – . £ (
RE-ALL AGENTS ACTIVE CALLING . – £ $ (
ALL RE-AGENTS ACTIVE CALLING – . £ $ (

RE-AGENTS ALL ACTIVE CALLING . £ – $ (
AGENTS RE-ALL ACTIVE CALLING £ . – $ (
ALL AGENTS RE-ACTIVE CALLING – £ . $ (
AGENTS ALL RE-ACTIVE CALLING £ – . $ (

RE-ACTIVE AGENTS ALL CALLING . $ £ – (
ACTIVE RE-AGENTS ALL CALLING $. £ – (
RE-AGENTS ACTIVE ALL CALLING . £ $ – (
AGENTS RE-ACTIVE ALL CALLING £ . $ – (

ACTIVE AGENTS RE-ALL CALLING $ £ . – (
AGENTS ACTIVE RE-ALL CALLING £ $. – (
ALL ACTIVE AGENTS RE-CALLING – $ £ . (
ACTIVE ALL AGENTS RE-CALLING $ – £ . (

ALL AGENTS ACTIVE RE-CALLING – £ $. (
AGENTS ALL ACTIVE RE-CALLING £ – $. (
ACTIVE AGENTS ALL RE-CALLING $ £ – . (
AGENTS ACTIVE ALL RE-CALLING £ $ – . (

RE-CALLING ACTIVE AGENTS ALL . ($ £ -
CALLING RE-ACTIVE AGENTS ALL (. $ £ -
RE-ACTIVE CALLING AGENTS ALL . $ (£ -
ACTIVE RE-CALLING AGENTS ALL $. (£ -

CALLING ACTIVE RE-AGENTS ALL ($. £ -
ACTIVE CALLING RE-AGENTS ALL $ (. £ -
RE-CALLING AGENTS ACTIVE ALL . (£ $ -
CALLING RE-AGENTS ACTIVE ALL (. £ $ -

RE-AGENTS CALLING ACTIVE ALL . £ ($ -
AGENTS RE-CALLING ACTIVE ALL £ . ($ -
CALLING AGENTS RE-ACTIVE ALL (£ . $ -
AGENTS CALLING RE-ACTIVE ALL £ (. $ -

RE-ACTIVE AGENTS CALLING ALL . $ £ (-
ACTIVE RE-AGENTS CALLING ALL $. £ (-
RE-AGENTS ACTIVE CALLING ALL . £ $ (-
AGENTS RE-ACTIVE CALLING ALL £ . $ (-

ACTIVE AGENTS RE-CALLING ALL $ £ . (-
AGENTS ACTIVE RE-CALLING ALL £ $. (-
CALLING ACTIVE AGENTS RE-ALL ($ £ . -
ACTIVE CALLING AGENTS RE-ALL $ (£ . -

CALLING AGENTS ACTIVE RE-ALL (£ $. -
AGENTS CALLING ACTIVE RE-ALL £ ($. -
ACTIVE AGENTS CALLING RE-ALL $ £ (. -
AGENTS ACTIVE CALLING RE-ALL £ $ (. -

ALL CALLING ACTIVE AGENTS RE- – ($ £ .
CALLING ALL ACTIVE AGENTS RE- (– $ £ .
ALL ACTIVE CALLING AGENTS RE- – $ (£ .
ACTIVE ALL CALLING AGENTS RE- $ – (£ .

CALLING ACTIVE ALL AGENTS RE- ($ – £ .
ACTIVE CALLING ALL AGENTS RE- $ (– £ .
ALL CALLING AGENTS ACTIVE RE- – (£ $.
CALLING ALL AGENTS ACTIVE RE- (– £ $.

ALL AGENTS CALLING ACTIVE RE- – £ ($.
AGENTS ALL CALLING ACTIVE RE- £ – ($.
CALLING AGENTS ALL ACTIVE RE- (£ – $.
AGENTS CALLING ALL ACTIVE RE- £ (– $.

ALL ACTIVE AGENTS CALLING RE- – $ £ (.
ACTIVE ALL AGENTS CALLING RE- $ – £ (.
ALL AGENTS ACTIVE CALLING RE- – £ $ (.
AGENTS ALL ACTIVE CALLING RE- £ – $ (.

ACTIVE AGENTS ALL CALLING RE- $ £ – (.
AGENTS ACTIVE ALL CALLING RE- £ $ – (.
CALLING ACTIVE AGENTS ALL RE- ($ £ – .
ACTIVE CALLING AGENTS ALL RE- $ (£ – .

CALLING AGENTS ACTIVE ALL RE- (£ $ – .
AGENTS CALLING ACTIVE ALL RE- £ ($ – .
ACTIVE AGENTS CALLING ALL RE- $ £ (– .
AGENTS ACTIVE CALLING ALL RE- £ $ (– .

I THINK THEREFORE I AM .   1 § ** 1 % .
I THINK THEREFORE I AM   1 § ** 1 . %
I THINK THEREFORE I AM   1 § ** . 1 %
I THINK . THEREFORE I AM   1 § . ** 1 %
I THEREFORE THINK I AM   1 . § ** 1 %
I THINK THEREFORE I AM   1 § ** 1 %

I THINK THEREFORE I AM .   1 § ** 1 % .
I THINK THEREFORE I .   1 § ** 1 % .
AM I THINK THEREFORE .   % 1 § ** .
I AM I THINK .   1 % 1 § .
THEREFORE I AM I .   ** 1 % 1 .
THEREFORE THINK I AM .   ** § 1 % .

I THINK THEREFORE I AM   1 § ** 1 %
I THINK I AM THEREFORE   1 § 1 % **
I THINK AM THEREFORE I   1 § % ** 1
I THINK THEREFORE AM I   1 § ** % 1
I THINK I THEREFORE AM   1 § 1 ** %
I THINK I AM THEREFORE   1 § 1 % **

I THEREFORE THINK I AM   1 ** § 1 %
I THEREFORE 1 THINK AM   1 ** 1 % §
I THEREFORE AM I THINK   1 ** % 1 §
I THEREFORE THINK AM I   1 ** § % 1
I THEREFORE I AM THINK   1 ** 1 % §
I THEREFORE AM THINK I   1 ** % § 1

THINK THEREFORE I AM I   § ** 1 % 1
THINK THEREFORE AM I I   § ** % 1 1
THINK THEREFORE I I AM   § ** 1 1 %

I AM I THINK THEREFORE   1 % 1 § **
I AM THINK I THEREFORE   1 % § 1 **
I AM THEREFORE THINK I   1 % ** § 1
I AM I THEREFORE THINK   1 % 1 ** §
I AM THINK THEREFORE I   1 % § ** 1
I AM THEREFORE I THINK   1 % ** 1 §

RUB OUT THE WRITE WORD
RUB OUT RIGHT WORD THEE
RUB OUT WORD RITE THEE
RUB OUT THE WORD RIGHT
RUB OUT RIGHT THE WORD
RUB OUT WORD THEE WRITE

RUB THE WORD RIGHT OUT
RUB THE RIGHT OUT WORD
RUB THE OUT WORD RIGHT
WORD OUT RIGHT
RIGHT WORD OUT
OUT RIGHT WORD

RUB WORD RIGHT OUT THE
RUB WORD OUT RIGHT THE
RUB WORD THE RIGHT OUT
RIGHT THE OUT
OUT THE RIGHT
THE OUT RIGHT

WORD RUB THE RIGHT OUT
RUB RIGHT OUT THE
OUT RIGHT THE
THE OUT RIGHT
RIGHT THE OUT
OUT THE RIGHT

WORD RIGHT RUB THE OUT
THE
OUT
RUB
THE
OUT

RUB OUT THE WORDS
RUB OUT THE
WORDS RUB OUT
THE WORDS RUB
OUT THE WORDS

RUB OUT THE WORDS
RUB THE WORDS OUT
RUB WORDS THEE OUT
RUB OUT WORDS THEE
RUB THE OUT WORDS
RUB WORDS OUT THEE

OUT THE WORDS RUB
OUT WORDS RUB THEE
OUT RUB WORDS THEE
OUT THEE RUB WORDS
OUT WORDS RUB THEE
OUT RUB THE WORDS

THE WORDS RUB OUT
THEE RUB WORDS OUT
THE OUT RUB WORDS
THE WORDS OUT RUB
THE RUB OUT WORDS
THE OUT WORDS RUB

WORDS RUB OUT THEE
WORDS OUT RUB THEE
WORDS THEE OUT RUB
WORDS RUB THEE OUT
WORDS OUT THEE RUB
WORDS THEE RUB OUT

RUB	OUT	THE	WORDS
#	$	%	&
#	$	%	
&	#	$	
%	&	#	
$	%	&	
#	$	%	&
#	%	&	$
#	&	%	$
#	$	&	%
#	%	$	&
#	&	$	%
$	%	&	#
$	&	#	%
$	#	&	%
$	%	#	&
$	&	#	%
$	#	%	&
%	&	#	$
%	#	&	$
%	$	#	&
%	&	$	#
%	#	$	&
%	$	&	#
&	#	$	%
&	$	#	%
&	%	$	#
&	$	%	#
&	$	%	#
&	%	#	$

				RUB OUT THE WORD			
RUB	OUT	THE	WORD	#	$	%	&
RUB	OUT	THE		#	$	%	
WORD	RUB	OUT		&	#	$	
THE	WORD	RUB		%	&	#	
OUT	THE	WORD		$	%	&	
RUB	OUT	THE	WORD	#	$	%	&
RUB	THE	WORD	OUT	#	%	&	$
RUB	WORD	THEE	OUT	#	&	%	$
RUB	OUT	WORD	THEE	#	$	&	%
RUB	THE	OUT	WORD	#	%	$	&
RUB	WORD	OUT	THEE	#	&	$	%
OUT	THE	WORD	RUB	$	%	&	#
OUT	WORD	RUB	THEE	$	&	#	%
OUT	RUB	WORD	THEE	$	#	&	%
OUT	THEE	RUB	WORD	$	%	#	&
OUT	WORD	RUB	THEE	$	&	#	%
OUT	RUB	THE	WORD	$	#	%	&
THE	WORD	RUB	OUT	%	&	#	$
THEE	RUB	WORD	OUT	%	#	&	$
THE	OUT	RUB	WORD	%	$	#	&
THE	WORD	OUT	RUB	%	&	$	#
THE	RUB	OUT	WORD	%	#	$	&
THE	OUT	WORD	RUB	%	$	&	#
WORD	RUB	OUT	THEE	&	#	$	%
WORD	OUT	RUB	THEE	&	$	#	%
WORD	THEE	OUT	RUB	&	%	$	#
WORD	RUB	THEE	OUT	&	$	%	#
WORD	OUT	THEE	RUB	&	$	%	#
WORD	THEE	RUB	OUT	&	%	#	$

WHO SENDS THE MAN
WHO SENDS THEE?
MAN WHO SENDS?
THE MAN WHO?
SENDS THE MAN

WHO SENDS THE MAN
WHO THE MAN SENDS
WHO MAN THE SENDS
WHO SENDS MAN THEE
WHO THEE SENDS MAN
WHO MAN SENDS THEE

SENDS THE MAN WHO
SENDS MAN THE WHO
SENDS WHO THE MAN
SENDS THEE WHO MAN
SENDS MAN WHO THEE
SENDS WHO MAN THEE

THE MAN WHO SENDS
THE WHO SENDS MAN
THE SENDS WHO MAN
THEE MAN SENDS WHO
THEE WHO MAN SENDS
THEE SENDS MAN WHO

MAN WHO SENDS THEE
MAN SENDS WHO THEE
MAN THEE WHO SENDS
MAN WHO THEE SENDS
MAN SENDS THEE WHO
MAN THEE SENDS WHO

WHO SENDS THE MAN ?
WHO SENDS THEE ?
MAN WHO SENDS ?
THE MAN WHO ?
SENDS THE MAN

? WHO SENDS THE MAN
WHO THE MAN SENDS
WHO MAN THE SENDS
WHO SENDS MAN THEE
WHO THEE SENDS MAN
WHO MAN SENDS THEE

MAKES THE MAN WHO
MAKES MAN THE WHO
MAKES WHO THE MAN
MAKES THEE WHO MAN
MAKES MAN WHO THE
MAKES WHO MAN THEE

THE MAN WHO SENDS
THE WHO SENDS MAN
THE SENDS MAN WHO
THE MAN SENDS WHO
THE WHO MAN SENDS
THE SENDS WHO MAN

MAN WHO SENDS THE
MAN MAKES WHO THE
MAN THE WHO SENDS
MAN WHO THE MAKES
MAN SENDS THE WHO
MAN THE MAKES WHO

KICK THAT HABIT MAN
KICK THAT HABIT
MAN KICK THAT
HABIT MAN KICK
THAT HABIT MAN

KICK THAT HABIT MAN
KICK HABIT THAT MAN
KICK MAN HABIT THAT
KICK THAT MAN HABIT
KICK HABIT MAN THAT
KICK MAN THAT HABIT

THAT HABIT KICK MAN
THAT KICK HABIT MAN
THAT MAN HABIT KICK
THAT HABIT MAN KICK
THAT KICK MAN HABIT
THAT MAN KICK HABIT

HABIT MAN KICK THAT
HABIT KICK THAT MAN
HABIT THAT MAN KICK
HABIT MAN THAT KICK
HABIT KICK MAN THAT
HABIT THAT KICK MAN

MAN KICK THAT HABIT
MAN THAT HABIT KICK
MAN HABIT KICK THAT
MAN KICK HABIT THAT
MAN THAT KICK HABIT
MAN HABIT THAT KICK

KICK THAT HABIT MAN
THAT HABIT KICK MAN
HABIT MAN KICK THAT
MAN KICK THAT HABIT

KICK MAN HABIT THAT
THAT HABIT MAN KICK
HABIT KICK THAT MAN
MAN KICK HABIT THAT

THAT KICK MAN HABIT
HABIT THAT KICK MAN
MAN THAT KICK HABIT
KICK MAN THAT HABIT

HABIT KICK MAN THAT
KICK HABIT MAN THAT
MAN HABIT THAT KICK
THAT MAN KICK HABIT

KICK THAT MAN HABIT
THAT MAN HABIT KICK
MAN HABIT KICK THAT
HABIT MAN THAT KICK

KICK THAT HABIT MAN
THAT HABIT KICK MAN
MAN KICK THAT HABIT
KICK THAT MAN HABIT

MAN HABIT KICK THAT
THAT KICK MAN HABIT
KICK HABIT MAN THAT
HABIT MAN KICK THAT

THAT KICK HABIT MAN
KICK HABIT THAT MAN
THAT HABIT MAN KICK
HABIT THAT MAN KICK

MAN THAT KICK HABIT
KICK MAN THAT HABIT
HABIT KICK THAT MAN
THAT MAN KICK HABIT

HABIT KICK MAN THAT
KICK MAN HABIT THAT
MAN KICK HABIT THAT
HABIT THAT KICK MAN

THAT MAN HABIT KICK
MAN THAT HABIT KICK
HABIT MAN THAT KICK
MAN HABIT THAT KICK

KICK THAT HABIT MAN   - ($ £
THAT KICK HABIT MAN   (- $ £
KICK HABIT THAT MAN   - $ (£
HABIT KICK THAT MAN $ - (£

THAT HABIT KICK MAN   ($ - £
HABIT THAT KICK MAN $ (- £
KICK THAT MAN HABIT   - (£ $
THAT KICK MAN HABIT   (- £ $

KICK MAN THAT HABIT   - £ ($
MAN KICK THAT HABIT   £ - ($
THAT MAN KICK HABIT   (£ - $
MAN THAT KICK HABIT   £ (- $

KICK HABIT MAN THAT   - $ £ (
HABIT KICK MAN THAT $ - £ (
KICK MAN HABIT THAT   - £ $ (
MAN KICK HABIT THAT   £ - $ (

HABIT MAN KICK THAT $ £ - (
MAN HABIT KICK THAT   £ $ - (
THAT HABIT MAN KICK   ($ £ -
HABIT THAT MAN KICK $ (£ -

THAT MAN HABIT KICK   (£ $ -
MAN THAT HABIT KICK   £ ($ -
HABIT MAN THAT KICK $ £ (-
MAN HABIT THAT KICK   £ $ (-

JUNK IS NO GOOD BABY
JUNK IS NO GOOD
BABY JUNK IS NO
NO GOOD BABY JUNK
IS NO GOOD BABY

JUNK IS NO GOOD BABY
JUNK IS GOOD - NO BABY
JUNK IS BABY - NO GOOD
JUNK IS NO BABY - GOOD
JUNK IS GOOD BABY - NO
JUNK IS BABY GOOD - NO

BABY IS NO GOOD - JUNK
BABY IS GOOD - NO JUNK
BABY IS JUNK - NO GOOD
BABY IS NO JUNK GOOD
BABY IS GOOD - JUNK NO
BABY IS JUNK GOOD - NO

IS NO GOOD BABY - JUNK
IS NO BABY JUNK GOOD
IS NO JUNK BABY GOOD
IS NO GOOD JUNK BABY
IS NO BABY - GOOD JUNK
IS NO JUNK GOOD BABY

IS GOOD BABY - NO JUNK
IS GOOD - NO JUNK BABY
IS GOOD JUNK - NO BABY
IS GOOD BABY - JUNK NO
IS GOOD NO BABY JUNK
IS GOOD JUNK BABY - NO

NO GOOD BABY IS JUNK
NO GOOD IS BABY JUNK
NO GOOD JUNK IS BABY
NO GOOD BABY JUNK IS
NO GOOD IS JUNK BABY
NO GOOD JUNK BABY IS

JUNK IS NO GOOD BABY
IS NO GOOD BABY JUNK
NO GOOD BABY IS JUNK
GOOD IS NO JUNK BABY
BABY IS NO GOOD JUNK

JUNK IS GOOD NO BABY
IS NO BABY JUNK GOOD
NO GOOD IS BABY JUNK
BABY IS GOOD NO JUNK
GOOD IS BABY JUNK NO

JUNK IS BABY NO GOOD
IS JUNK BABY NO GOOD
NO GOOD IS JUNK BABY
JUNK BABY IS NO GOOD
GOOD BABY IS JUNK NO

JUNK IS NO GOOD BABY　IS JUNK NO GOOD BABY　– • ($ £
JUNK NO IS GOOD BABY　NO JUNK IS GOOD BABY　(• – $ £
IS NO JUNK GOOD BABY　NO IS JUNK GOOD BABY　(– • $ £
JUNK IS GOOD NO BABY　IS JUNK GOOD NO BABY　– • $ (£
JUNK GOOD IS NO BABY　GOOD JUNK IS NO BABY　$ • – (£
IS GOOD JUNK NO BABY　GOOD IS JUNK NO BABY　$ – • (£
JUNK NO GOOD IS BABY　NO JUNK GOOD IS BABY　(• $ – £
JUNK GOOD NO IS BABY　GOOD JUNK NO IS BABY　$ • (– £
NO GOOD JUNK IS BABY　GOOD NO JUNK IS BABY　$ (• – £
IS NO GOOD JUNK BABY　NO IS GOOD JUNK BABY　(– $ • £
IS GOOD NO JUNK BABY　GOOD IS NO JUNK BABY　$ – (• £
NO GOOD IS JUNK BABY　GOOD NO IS JUNK BABY　$ (– • £
JUNK IS NO BABY GOOD　IS JUNK NO BABY GOOD　– • (£ $
JUNK NO IS BABY GOOD　NO JUNK IS BABY GOOD　(• – £ $
IS NO JUNK BABY GOOD　NO IS JUNK BABY GOOD　(– • £ $
JUNK IS BABY NO GOOD　IS JUNK BABY NO GOOD　– • £ ($
JUNK BABY IS NO GOOD　BABY JUNK IS NO GOOD　£ • – ($
IS BABY JUNK NO GOOD　BABY IS JUNK NO GOOD　£ – • ($
JUNK NO BABY IS GOOD　NO JUNK BABY IS GOOD　(• £ – $
JUNK BABY NO IS GOOD　BABY JUNK NO IS GOOD　£ • (– $
NO BABY JUNK IS GOOD　BABY NO JUNK IS GOOD　£ (• – $
IS NO BABY JUNK GOOD　NO IS BABY JUNK GOOD　(– £ • $
IS BABY NO JUNK GOOD　BABY IS NO JUNK GOOD　£ – (• $
NO BABY IS JUNK GOOD　BABY NO IS JUNK GOOD　£ (– • $
JUNK IS GOOD BABY NO　IS JUNK GOOD BABY NO　– • $ £ (
JUNK GOOD IS BABY NO　GOOD JUNK IS BABY NO　$ • – £ (
IS GOOD JUNK BABY NO　GOOD IS JUNK BABY NO　$ – • £ (
JUNK IS BABY GOOD NO　IS JUNK BABY GOOD NO　– • £ $ (
JUNK BABY IS GOOD NO　BABY JUNK IS GOOD NO　£ • – $ (
IS BABY JUNK GOOD NO　BABY IS JUNK GOOD NO　£ – • $ (
JUNK GOOD BABY IS NO　GOOD JUNK BABY IS NO　$ • £ – (
JUNK BABY GOOD IS NO　BABY JUNK GOOD IS NO　£ • $ – (
GOOD BABY JUNK IS NO　BABY GOOD JUNK IS NO　£ $ • – (
IS GOOD BABY JUNK NO　GOOD IS BABY JUNK NO　$ – £ • (
IS BABY GOOD JUNK NO　BABY IS GOOD JUNK NO　£ – $ • (
GOOD BABY IS JUNK NO　BABY GOOD IS JUNK NO　£ $ – • (
JUNK NO GOOD BABY IS　NO JUNK GOOD BABY IS　(• $ £ –
JUNK GOOD NO BABY IS　GOOD JUNK NO BABY IS　$ • (£ –
NO GOOD JUNK BABY IS　GOOD NO JUNK BABY IS　$ (• £ –
JUNK NO BABY GOOD IS　NO JUNK BABY GOOD IS　(• £ $ –
JUNK BABY NO GOOD IS　BABY JUNK NO GOOD IS　£ • ($ –
NO BABY JUNK GOOD IS　BABY NO JUNK GOOD IS　£ (• $ –
JUNK GOOD BABY NO IS　GOOD JUNK BABY NO IS　$ • £ (–
JUNK BABY GOOD NO IS　BABY JUNK GOOD NO IS　£ • $ (–
GOOD BABY JUNK NO IS　BABY GOOD JUNK NO IS　£ $ • (–
NO GOOD BABY JUNK IS　GOOD NO BABY JUNK IS　$ (£ • –
NO BABY GOOD JUNK IS　BABY NO GOOD JUNK IS　£ ($ • –
GOOD BABY NO JUNK IS　BABY GOOD NO JUNK IS　£ $ (• –
IS NO GOOD BABY JUNK　NO IS GOOD BABY JUNK　(– $ £ •
IS GOOD NO BABY JUNK　GOOD IS NO BABY JUNK　$ – (£ •
NO GOOD IS BABY JUNK　GOOD NO IS BABY JUNK　$ (– £ •
IS NO BABY GOOD JUNK　NO IS BABY GOOD JUNK　(– £ $ •
IS BABY NO GOOD JUNK　BABY IS NO GOOD JUNK　£ – ($ •
NO BABY IS GOOD JUNK　BABY NO IS GOOD JUNK　£ (– $ •
IS GOOD BABY NO JUNK　GOOD IS BABY NO JUNK　$ – £ (•
IS BABY GOOD NO JUNK　BABY IS GOOD NO JUNK　£ – $ (•
GOOD BABY IS NO JUNK　BABY GOOD IS NO JUNK　£ $ – (•
NO GOOD BABY IS JUNK　GOOD NO BABY IS JUNK　$ (£ – •
NO BABY GOOD IS JUNK　BABY NO GOOD IS JUNK　£ ($ – •
GOOD BABY NO IS JUNK　BABY GOOD NO IS JUNK　£ $ (– •

CAN MOTHER BE WRONG?
CAN MOTHER BE?
WRONG CAN MOTHER?
BE WRONG CAN?
MOTHER BEE WRONG

CAN MOTHER BE WRONG
CAN BE MOTHER WRONG
CAN WRONG BE MOTHER
CAN MOTHER WRONG BE
CAN BE WRONG MOTHER
CAN WRONG MOTHER BE

MOTHER CAN BE WRONG
MOTHER BE GAN WRONG
MOTHER WRONG BEGAN
MOTHER CAN WRONG BE
MOTHER BE WRONG CAN
MOTHER WRONG CAN BE

BE WRONG CAN MOTHER
BEGAN WRONG MOTHER
BEE MOTHER WRONG CAN
BE WRONG MOTHER CAN
BEGAN MOTHER WRONG
BEE MOTHER CAN WRONG

WRONG BEGAN MOTHER
WRONG CAN MOTHER BE
WRONG MOTHER CAN BE
WRONG BEE MOTHER CAN
WRONG CAN BEE MOTHER
WRONG MOTHER BEGAN

SHORT TIME TO GO
SHORT TIME TOO
GO SHORT TIME
TO GO SHORT
TIME TO GO

SHORT TIME TO GO
SHORT TO GO TIME
SHORT GO TO TIME
SHORT TIME GO TOO
SHORT TOO TIME GO
SHORT GO TOO TIME

TIME TO GO SHORT
TIME GO SHORT TO
TIME SHORT TO GO
TIME TOO SHORT GO
TIME GO TOO SHORT
TIME SHORT GO TOO

TO GO SHORT TIME
TO SHORT GO TIME
TO TIME GO SHORT
TWO GO TIME SHORT
TWO SHORT TIME GO
TWO TIME SHORT GO

GO TIME TOO SHORT
GO TWO TIME SHORT
GO SHORT TWO TIME
GO TIME SHORT TOO
GO TOO SHORT TIME
GO SHORT TIME TOO

IN THE BEGINNING WAS THE WORD
IN THE BEGINNING WAS THEE
WORD IN THEE BEGINNING WAS
THE WORD IN THEE BEGINNING
WAS THE WORD IN THEE
BEGINNING WAS THE WORD IN
THEE BEGINNING WAS THE WORD

IN THE BEGINNING WAS THE WORD
IN THE BEGINNING THE WAS WORD
IN THE BEGINNING WORD THE WAS
IN THE BEGINNING WAS WORD THE
IN THE BEGINNING THE WORD WAS
IN THE BEGINNING WORD WAS THEE

IN THE BEGINNING WAS THE WORD
THE IN BEGINNING THE WAS WORD
BEGINNING THE IN WORD THE WAS
IN BEGINNING THE WAS WORD THE
THE BEGINNING IN THE WORD WAS
BEGINNING IN THE WORD WAS THE

THE BEGINNING WAS THE WORD IN
THE BEGINNING WAS IN THE WORD

BEGINNING WAS THE WORD IN THE
BEGINNING WAS THE THE IN WORD

WAS THE WORD IN THE BEGINNING
WAS THE WORD BEGINNING IN THE

WORD THE IN BEGINNING WAS THE
WORD THE IN THE BEGINNING WAS

THE BEGINNING WORD THE WAS IN
THE BEGINNING WORD IN THE WAS

THE BEGINNING THE IN WAS WORD
THE BEGINNING THE WORD WAS IN

THE IN WORD THE WAS BEGINNING
THE IN WORD WAS BEGINNING THE

IN WORD BEGINNING WAS THE THE
IN WORD BEGINNING THE WAS THE

IN THE WAS THE BEGINNING WORD
IN THE WAS WORD BEGINNING THE

IN WAS WORD BEGINNING THE THE
IN WAS WORD THE THE BEGINNING

THE BEGINNING WAS THE WORD IN

IN THE BEGINNING WAS THE WORD .
IN THE BEGINNING WAS THEE .
WORD IN THE BEGINNING WAS .
THE WORD IN THE BEGINNING .
WAS THE WORD IN THE .
BEGINNING WAS THE WORD IN .
THEE BEGINNING WAS THE WORD

IN THE BEGINNING WAS THE WORD
IN THE BEGINNING THE WAS WORD
IN THE BEGINNING WORD THE WAS
IN THE BEGINNING WAS WORD THE
IN THE BEGINNING THE WAS WORD
IN THE BEGINNING WORD WAS THE

IN THE BEGINNING WAS THE WORD
THE IN BEGINNING WAS THE WORD
BEGINNING THE IN WAS THE WORD
IN BEGINNING THE WAS THE WORD
THE BEGINNING IN WAS THE WORD
BEGINNING IN THE WAS THE WORD

IN THE BEGINNING THE WAS WORD
THE IN BEGINNING THE WAS WORD
BEGINNING THE IN THE WAS WORD
IN BEGINNING THE THE WAS WORD
THE BEGINNING IN THE WAS WORD
BEGINNING IN THE THE WAS WORD

IN THE BEGINNING WORD THE WAS
THE IN BEGINNING WORD THE WAS
BEGINNING THE IN WORD THE WAS
IN BEGINNING THE WORD THE WAS
THE BEGINNING IN WORD THE WAS
BEGINNING IN THE WORD THE WAS

IN	THE	BEGINNING	WAS	WORD	THE
THE	IN	BEGINNING	WAS	WORD	THE
BEGINNING	THE	IN	WAS	WORD	THE
IN	BEGINNING	THE	WAS	WORD	THE
THE	BEGINNING	IN	WAS	WORD	THE
BEGINNING	IN	THE	WAS	WORD	THE

IN	THE	BEGINNING	THE	WORD	WAS
THE	IN	BEGINNING	THE	WORD	WAS
BEGINNING	THE	IN	THE	WORD	WAS
IN	BEGINNING	THE	THE	WORD	WAS
THE	BEGINNING	IN	THE	WORD	WAS
BEGINNING	IN	THE	THE	WORD	WAS

IN	THE	BEGINNING	WORD	WAS	THE
THE	IN	BEGINNING	WORD	WAS	THE
BEGINNING	THE	IN	WORD	WAS	THE
IN	BEGINNING	THE	WORD	WAS	THE
THE	BEGINNING	IN	WORD	WAS	THE
BEGINNING	IN	THE	WORD	WAS	THE

THE	BEGINNING	WAS	THE	WORD	IN
			WORD	THE	IN
			IN	THE	WORD
			THE	IN	WORD
			WORD	IN	THE
			IN	WORD	THE

BEGINNING	WAS	THE	WORD	IN	THE
			IN	THE	WORD
			THE	WORD	IN
			WORD	THE	IN
			IN	WORD	THE
			THE	IN	WORD

WAS	THE	WORD	IN	THE	BEGINNING
			THE	BEGINNING	IN
			BEGINNING	THE	IN
			IN	BEGINNING	THE
			THE	IN	BEGINNING
			BEGINNING	IN	THE

WORD	THE	IN	BEGINNING	WAS	THE
			WAS	THE	BEGINNING
			THE	WAS	BEGINNING
			BEGINNING	THE	WAS
			WAS	BEGINNING	THE
			THE	BEGINNING	WAS
THE	BEGINNING	WORD	THE	WAS	IN
			WAS	THE	IN
			IN	WAS	THE
			THE	IN	WAS
			WAS	IN	THE
			IN	THE	WAS
THE	BEGINNING	THE	IN	WAS	WORD
			WAS	IN	WORD
			WORD	IN	WAS
			IN	WORD	WAS
			WAS	WORD	IN
			WORD	WAS	IN
THE	IN	WORD	THE	WAS	BEGINNING
			WAS	THE	BEGINNING
			BEGINNING	THE	WAS
			THE	BEGINNING	WAS
			BEGINNING	WAS	THE
			WAS	BEGINNING	THE
THE	THE	WORD	WAS	IN	BEGINNING
			IN	BEGINNING	WAS
			BEGINNING	IN	WAS
			IN	WAS	BEGINNING
			BEGINNING	WAS	IN
			WAS	BEGINNING	IN
IN	WORD	BEGINNING	WAS	THE	THE
			THE	WAS	THE
			THE	THE	WAS
			WAS	THE	THE
			THE	WAS	THE
			THE	WAS	THE

IN	THE	WAS	THE	BEGINNING	WORD
			BEGINNING	WORD	THE
			WORD	THE	BEGINNING
			THE	WORD	BEGINNING
			BEGINNING	THE	WORD
			WORD	BEGINNING	THE
IN	WAS	WORD	THE	BEGINNING	THE
			BEGINNING	THE	THE
			THE	BEGINNING	WORD
			THE	THE	BEGINNING
			BEGINNING	THE	THE
			THE	THE	BEGINNING
THEE	BEGINNING	WAS	THEE	WORD	IN

IN THE BEGINNING WAS THE WORD
THE IN BEGINNING WAS THE WORD
IN BEGINNING THEE WAS THE WORD
BEGINNING IN THEE WAS THE WORD
THE BEGINNING IN WAS THE WORD
BEGINNING THEE IN WAS THE WORD

IN THEE WAS BEGINNING THE WORD
THEE IN WAS BEGINNING THE WORD
IN WAS THE BEGINNING THE WORD
WAS IN THE BEGINNING THE WORD
THEE WAS IN BEGINNING THE WORD
WAS THEE IN BEGINNING THE WORD

IN BEGINNING WAS THEE THE WORD
BEGINNING IN WAS THEE THE WORD
IN WAS BEGINNING THEE THE WORD
WAS IN BEGINNING THEE THE WORD
BEGINNING WAS IN THEE THE WORD
WAS BEGINNING IN THEE THE WORD

THE BEGINNING WAS IN THE WORD
BEGINNING THEE WAS IN THE WORD
THEE WAS BEGINNING IN THE WORD
WAS THE BEGINNING IN THE WORD
BEGINNING WAS THEE IN THE WORD
WAS BEGINNING THEE IN THE WORD

IN THE BEGINNING THEE WAS WORD
THEE IN BEGINNING THEE WAS WORD
IN BEGINNING THEE THEE WAS WORD
BEGINNING IN THEE THEE WAS WORD
THE BEGINNING IN THEE WAS WORD
BEGINNING THEE IN THEE WAS WORD

IN THE BEGINNING

IN THE BEGINNING WORD THEE WAS
THE BEGINNING IN WORD THEE WAS
BEGINNING IN THEE WORD THEE WAS

IN THE BEGINNING WAS WORD THEE
THE IN BEGINNING WAS WORD THEE
BEGINNING THEE IN WAS WORD THEE
IN BEGINNING THEE WAS WORD THEE
THE BEGINNING IN WAS WORD THEE
BEGINNING IN THEE WAS WORD THEE

IN THE BEGINNING THEE WORD WAS
THEE IN BEGINNING THEE WORD WAS
BEGINNING THEE IN THEE WORD WAS
IN BEGINNING THEE THEE WORD WAS
THE BEGINNING IN THEE WORD WAS
BEGINNING IN THEE THEE WORD WAS

IN THE BEGINNING WAS THE WORD
THE IN BEGINNING WAS THE WORD
IN BEGINNING THE WAS THE WORD
BEGINNING IN THE WAS THE WORD
THE BEGINNING IN WAS THE WORD
BEGINNING THE IN WAS THE WORD
IN THE WAS BEGINNING THE WORD
THE IN WAS BEGINNING THE WORD
IN WAS THE BEGINNING THE WORD
WAS IN THE BEGINNING THE WORD
THE WAS IN BEGINNING THE WORD
WAS THE IN BEGINNING THE WORD
IN BEGINNING WAS THE THE WORD
BEGINNING IN WAS THE THE WORD
IN WAS BEGINNING THE THE WORD
WAS IN BEGINNING THE THE WORD
BEGINNING WAS IN THE THE WORD
WAS BEGINNING IN THE THE WORD
THE BEGINNING WAS IN THE WORD
BEGINNING THE WAS IN THE WORD
THE WAS BEGINNING IN THE WORD
WAS THE BEGINNING IN THE WORD
BEGINNING WAS THE IN THE WORD
WAS BEGINNING THE IN THE WORD
IN THE BEGINNING THE WAS WORD
THE IN BEGINNING THE WAS WORD
IN BEGINNING THE THE WAS WORD
BEGINNING IN THE THE WAS WORD
THE BEGINNING IN THE WAS WORD
BEGINNING THE IN THE WAS WORD
IN THE THE BEGINNING WAS WORD
THE IN THE BEGINNING WAS WORD
IN THE THE BEGINNING WAS WORD
THE IN THE BEGINNING WAS WORD
THE THE IN BEGINNING WAS WORD
THE THE IN BEGINNING WAS WORD
IN BEGINNING THE THE WAS WORD
BEGINNING IN THE THE WAS WORD
IN THE BEGINNING THE WAS WORD
THE IN BEGINNING THE WAS WORD
BEGINNING THE IN THE WAS WORD
THE BEGINNING IN THE WAS WORD
THE BEGINNING THE IN WAS WORD
BEGINNING THE THE IN WAS WORD
THE THE BEGINNING IN WAS WORD
THE THE BEGINNING IN WAS WORD
BEGINNING THE THE IN WAS WORD
THE BEGINNING THE IN WAS WORD
IN THE WAS THE BEGINNING WORD
THE IN WAS THE BEGINNING WORD
IN WAS THE THE BEGINNING WORD
WAS IN THE THE BEGINNING WORD
THE WAS IN THE BEGINNING WORD
WAS THE IN THE BEGINNING WORD
IN THE THE WAS BEGINNING WORD
THE IN THE WAS BEGINNING WORD
IN THE THE WAS BEGINNING WORD
THE IN THE WAS BEGINNING WORD
THE THE IN WAS BEGINNING WORD
THE THE IN WAS BEGINNING WORD

IN WAS THE THE BEGINNING WORD
WAS IN THE THE BEGINNING WORD
IN THE WAS THE BEGINNING WORD
THE IN WAS THE BEGINNING WORD
WAS THE IN THE BEGINNING WORD
THE WAS IN THE BEGINNING WORD
THE WAS THE IN BEGINNING WORD
WAS THE THE IN BEGINNING WORD
THE THE WAS IN BEGINNING WORD
THE THE WAS IN BEGINNING WORD
WAS THE THE IN BEGINNING WORD
THE WAS THE IN BEGINNING WORD
IN BEGINNING WAS THE THE WORD
BEGINNING IN WAS THE THE WORD
IN WAS BEGINNING THE THE WORD
WAS IN BEGINNING THE THE WORD
BEGINNING WAS IN THE THE WORD
WAS BEGINNING IN THE THE WORD
IN BEGINNING THE WAS THE WORD
BEGINNING IN THE WAS THE WORD
IN THE BEGINNING WAS THE WORD
THE IN BEGINNING WAS THE WORD
BEGINNING THE IN WAS THE WORD
THE BEGINNING IN WAS THE WORD
IN WAS THE BEGINNING THE WORD
WAS IN THE BEGINNING THE WORD
IN THE WAS BEGINNING THE WORD
THE IN WAS BEGINNING THE WORD
WAS THE IN BEGINNING THE WORD
THE WAS IN BEGINNING THE WORD
BEGINNING WAS THE IN THE WORD
WAS BEGINNING THE IN THE WORD
BEGINNING THE WAS IN THE WORD
THE BEGINNING WAS IN THE WORD
WAS THE BEGINNING IN THE WORD
THE WAS BEGINNING IN THE WORD
THE BEGINNING WAS THE IN WORD
BEGINNING THE WAS THE IN WORD
THE WAS BEGINNING THE IN WORD
WAS THE BEGINNING THE IN WORD
BEGINNING WAS THE THE IN WORD
WAS BEGINNING THE THE IN WORD
THE BEGINNING THE WAS IN WORD
BEGINNING THE THE WAS IN WORD
THE THE BEGINNING WAS IN WORD
THE THE BEGINNING WAS IN WORD
BEGINNING THE THE WAS IN WORD
THE BEGINNING THE WAS IN WORD
THE WAS THE BEGINNING IN WORD
WAS THE THE BEGINNING IN WORD
THE THE WAS BEGINNING IN WORD
THE THE WAS BEGINNING IN WORD
WAS THE THE BEGINNING IN WORD
THE WAS THE BEGINNING IN WORD
BEGINNING WAS THE THE IN WORD
WAS BEGINNING THE THE IN WORD
BEGINNING THE WAS THE IN WORD
THE BEGINNING WAS THE IN WORD
WAS THE BEGINNING THE IN WORD
THE WAS BEGINNING THE IN WORD

IN THE BEGINNING WAS WORD THE
THE IN BEGINNING WAS WORD THE
IN BEGINNING THE WAS WORD THE
BEGINNING IN THE WAS WORD THE
THE BEGINNING IN WAS WORD THE
BEGINNING THE IN WAS WORD THE
IN THE WAS BEGINNING WORD THE
THE IN WAS BEGINNING WORD THE
IN WAS THE BEGINNING WORD THE
WAS IN THE BEGINNING WORD THE
THE WAS IN BEGINNING WORD THE
WAS THE IN BEGINNING WORD THE
IN BEGINNING WAS THE WORD THE
BEGINNING IN WAS THE WORD THE
IN WAS BEGINNING THE WORD THE
WAS IN BEGINNING THE WORD THE
BEGINNING WAS IN THE WORD THE
WAS BEGINNING IN THE WORD THE
THE BEGINNING WAS IN WORD THE
BEGINNING THE WAS IN WORD THE
THE WAS BEGINNING IN WORD THE
WAS THE BEGINNING IN WORD THE
BEGINNING WAS THE IN WORD THE
WAS BEGINNING THE IN WORD THE
IN THE BEGINNING WORD WAS THE
THE IN BEGINNING WORD WAS THE
IN BEGINNING THE WORD WAS THE
BEGINNING IN THE WORD WAS THE
THE BEGINNING IN WORD WAS THE
BEGINNING THE IN WORD WAS THE
IN THE WORD BEGINNING WAS THE
THE IN WORD BEGINNING WAS THE
IN WORD THE BEGINNING WAS THE
WORD IN THE BEGINNING WAS THE
THE WORD IN BEGINNING WAS THE
WORD THE IN BEGINNING WAS THE
IN BEGINNING WORD THE WAS THE
BEGINNING IN WORD THE WAS THE
IN WORD BEGINNING THE WAS THE
WORD IN BEGINNING THE WAS THE
BEGINNING WORD IN THE WAS THE
WORD BEGINNING IN THE WAS THE
THE BEGINNING WORD IN WAS THE
BEGINNING THE WORD IN WAS THE
THE WORD BEGINNING IN WAS THE
WORD THE BEGINNING IN WAS THE
BEGINNING WORD THE IN WAS THE
WORD BEGINNING THE IN WAS THE
IN THE WAS WORD BEGINNING THE
THE IN WAS WORD BEGINNING THE
IN WAS THE WORD BEGINNING THE
WAS IN THE WORD BEGINNING THE
THE WAS IN WORD BEGINNING THE
WAS THE IN WORD BEGINNING THE
IN THE WORD WAS BEGINNING THE
THE IN WORD WAS BEGINNING THE
IN WORD THE WAS BEGINNING THE
WORD IN THE WAS BEGINNING THE
THE WORD IN WAS BEGINNING THE
WORD THE IN WAS BEGINNING THE

IN WAS WORD THE BEGINNING THE
WAS IN WORD THE BEGINNING THE
IN WORD WAS THE BEGINNING THE
WORD IN WAS THE BEGINNING THE
WAS WORD IN THE BEGINNING THE
WORD WAS IN THE BEGINNING THE
THE WAS WORD IN BEGINNING THE
WAS THE WORD IN BEGINNING THE
THE WORD WAS IN BEGINNING THE
WORD THE WAS IN BEGINNING THE
WAS WORD THE IN BEGINNING THE
WORD WAS THE IN BEGINNING THE
IN BEGINNING WAS WORD THE THE
BEGINNING IN WAS WORD THE THE
IN WAS BEGINNING WORD THE THE
WAS IN BEGINNING WORD THE THE
BEGINNING WAS IN WORD THE THE
WAS BEGINNING IN WORD THE THE
IN BEGINNING WORD WAS THE THE
BEGINNING IN WORD WAS THE THE
IN WORD BEGINNING WAS THE THE
WORD IN BEGINNING WAS THE THE
BEGINNING WORD IN WAS THE THE
WORD BEGINNING IN WAS THE THE
IN WAS WORD BEGINNING THE THE
WAS IN WORD BEGINNING THE THE
IN WORD WAS BEGINNING THE THE
WORD IN WAS BEGINNING THE THE
WAS WORD IN BEGINNING THE THE
WORD WAS IN BEGINNING THE THE
BEGINNING WAS WORD IN THE THE
WAS BEGINNING WORD IN THE THE
BEGINNING WORD WAS IN THE THE
WORD BEGINNING WAS IN THE THE
WAS WORD BEGINNING IN THE THE
WORD WAS BEGINNING IN THE THE
THE BEGINNING WAS WORD IN THE
BEGINNING THE WAS WORD IN THE
THE WAS BEGINNING WORD IN THE
WAS THE BEGINNING WORD IN THE
BEGINNING WAS THE WORD IN THE
WAS BEGINNING THE WORD IN THE
THE BEGINNING WORD WAS IN THE
BEGINNING THE WORD WAS IN THE
THE WORD BEGINNING WAS IN THE
WORD THE BEGINNING WAS IN THE
BEGINNING WORD THE WAS IN THE
WORD BEGINNING THE WAS IN THE
THE WAS WORD BEGINNING IN THE
WAS THE WORD BEGINNING IN THE
THE WORD WAS BEGINNING IN THE
WORD THE WAS BEGINNING IN THE
WAS WORD THE BEGINNING IN THE
WORD WAS THE BEGINNING IN THE
BEGINNING WAS WORD THE IN THE
WAS BEGINNING WORD THE IN THE
BEGINNING WORD WAS THE IN THE
WORD BEGINNING WAS THE IN THE
WAS WORD BEGINNING THE IN THE
WORD WAS BEGINNING THE IN THE

IN THE BEGINNING THE WORD WAS
THE IN BEGINNING THE WORD WAS
IN BEGINNING THE THE WORD WAS
BEGINNING IN THE THE WORD WAS
THE BEGINNING IN THE WORD WAS
BEGINNING THE IN THE WORD WAS
IN THE THE BEGINNING WORD WAS
THE IN THE BEGINNING WORD WAS
IN THE THE BEGINNING WORD WAS
THE IN THE BEGINNING WORD WAS
THE THE IN BEGINNING WORD WAS
THE THE IN BEGINNING WORD WAS
IN BEGINNING THE THE WORD WAS
BEGINNING IN THE THE WORD WAS
IN THE BEGINNING THE WORD WAS
THE IN BEGINNING THE WORD WAS
BEGINNING THE IN THE WORD WAS
THE BEGINNING IN THE WORD WAS
THE BEGINNING THE IN WORD WAS
BEGINNING THE THE IN WORD WAS
THE THE BEGINNING IN WORD WAS
THE THE BEGINNING IN WORD WAS
BEGINNING THE THE IN WORD WAS
THE BEGINNING THE IN WORD WAS
IN THE BEGINNING WORD THE WAS
THE IN BEGINNING WORD THE WAS
IN BEGINNING THE WORD THE WAS
BEGINNING IN THE WORD THE WAS
THE BEGINNING IN WORD THE WAS
BEGINNING THE IN WORD THE WAS
IN THE WORD BEGINNING THE WAS
THE IN WORD BEGINNING THE WAS
IN WORD THE BEGINNING THE WAS
WORD IN THE BEGINNING THE WAS
THE WORD IN BEGINNING THE WAS
WORD THE IN BEGINNING THE WAS
IN BEGINNING WORD THE THE WAS
BEGINNING IN WORD THE THE WAS
IN WORD BEGINNING THE THE WAS
WORD IN BEGINNING THE THE WAS
BEGINNING WORD IN THE THE WAS
WORD BEGINNING IN THE THE WAS
THE BEGINNING WORD IN THE WAS
BEGINNING THE WORD IN THE WAS
THE WORD BEGINNING IN THE WAS
WORD THE BEGINNING IN THE WAS
BEGINNING WORD THE IN THE WAS
WORD BEGINNING THE IN THE WAS
IN THE THE WORD BEGINNING WAS
THE IN THE WORD BEGINNING WAS
IN THE THE WORD BEGINNING WAS
THE IN THE WORD BEGINNING WAS
THE THE IN WORD BEGINNING WAS
THE THE IN WORD BEGINNING WAS
IN THE WORD THE BEGINNING WAS
THE IN WORD THE BEGINNING WAS
IN WORD THE THE BEGINNING WAS
WORD IN THE THE BEGINNING WAS
THE WORD IN THE BEGINNING WAS
WORD THE IN THE BEGINNING WAS

IN THE WORD THE BEGINNING WAS
THE IN WORD THE BEGINNING WAS
IN WORD THE THE BEGINNING WAS
WORD IN THE THE BEGINNING WAS
THE WORD IN THE BEGINNING WAS
WORD THE IN THE BEGINNING WAS
THE THE WORD IN BEGINNING WAS
THE THE WORD IN BEGINNING WAS
THE WORD THE IN BEGINNING WAS
WORD THE THE IN BEGINNING WAS
THE WORD THE IN BEGINNING WAS
WORD THE THE IN BEGINNING WAS
IN BEGINNING THE WORD THE WAS
BEGINNING IN THE WORD THE WAS
IN THE BEGINNING WORD THE WAS
THE IN BEGINNING WORD THE WAS
BEGINNING THE IN WORD THE WAS
THE BEGINNING IN WORD THE WAS
IN BEGINNING WORD THE THE WAS
BEGINNING IN WORD THE THE WAS
IN WORD BEGINNING THE THE WAS
WORD IN BEGINNING THE THE WAS
BEGINNING WORD IN THE THE WAS
WORD BEGINNING IN THE THE WAS
IN THE WORD BEGINNING THE WAS
THE IN WORD BEGINNING THE WAS
IN WORD THE BEGINNING THE WAS
WORD IN THE BEGINNING THE WAS
THE WORD IN BEGINNING THE WAS
WORD THE IN BEGINNING THE WAS
BEGINNING THE WORD IN THE WAS
THE BEGINNING WORD IN THE WAS
BEGINNING WORD THE IN THE WAS
WORD BEGINNING THE IN THE WAS
THE WORD BEGINNING IN THE WAS
WORD THE BEGINNING IN THE WAS
THE BEGINNING THE WORD IN WAS
BEGINNING THE THE WORD IN WAS
THE THE BEGINNING WORD IN WAS
THE THE BEGINNING WORD IN WAS
BEGINNING THE THE WORD IN WAS
THE BEGINNING THE WORD IN WAS
THE BEGINNING WORD THE IN WAS
BEGINNING THE WORD THE IN WAS
THE WORD BEGINNING THE IN WAS
WORD THE BEGINNING THE IN WAS
BEGINNING WORD THE THE IN WAS
WORD BEGINNING THE THE IN WAS
THE THE WORD BEGINNING IN WAS
THE THE WORD BEGINNING IN WAS
THE WORD THE BEGINNING IN WAS
WORD THE THE BEGINNING IN WAS
THE WORD THE BEGINNING IN WAS
WORD THE THE BEGINNING IN WAS
BEGINNING THE WORD THE IN WAS
THE BEGINNING WORD THE IN WAS
BEGINNING WORD THE THE IN WAS
WORD BEGINNING THE THE IN WAS
THE WORD BEGINNING THE IN WAS
WORD THE BEGINNING THE IN WAS

IN THE WAS THE WORD BEGINNING
THE IN WAS THE WORD BEGINNING
IN WAS THE THE WORD BEGINNING
WAS IN THE THE WORD BEGINNING
THE WAS IN THE WORD BEGINNING
WAS THE IN THE WORD BEGINNING
IN THE THE WAS WORD BEGINNING
THE IN THE WAS WORD BEGINNING
IN THE THE WAS WORD BEGINNING
THE IN THE WAS WORD BEGINNING
THE THE IN WAS WORD BEGINNING
THE THE IN WAS WORD BEGINNING
IN WAS THE THE WORD BEGINNING
WAS IN THE THE WORD BEGINNING
IN THE WAS THE WORD BEGINNING
THE IN WAS THE WORD BEGINNING
WAS THE IN THE WORD BEGINNING
THE WAS IN THE WORD BEGINNING
THE WAS THE IN WORD BEGINNING
WAS THE THE IN WORD BEGINNING
THE THE WAS IN WORD BEGINNING
THE THE WAS IN WORD BEGINNING
WAS THE THE IN WORD BEGINNING
THE WAS THE IN WORD BEGINNING
IN THE WAS WORD THE BEGINNING
THE IN WAS WORD THE BEGINNING
IN WAS THE WORD THE BEGINNING
WAS IN THE WORD THE BEGINNING
THE WAS IN WORD THE BEGINNING
WAS THE IN WORD THE BEGINNING
IN THE WORD WAS THE BEGINNING
THE IN WORD WAS THE BEGINNING
IN WORD THE WAS THE BEGINNING
WORD IN THE WAS THE BEGINNING
THE WORD IN WAS THE BEGINNING
WORD THE IN WAS THE BEGINNING
IN WAS WORD THE THE BEGINNING
WAS IN WORD THE THE BEGINNING
IN WORD WAS THE THE BEGINNING
WORD IN WAS THE THE BEGINNING
WAS WORD IN THE THE BEGINNING
WORD WAS IN THE THE BEGINNING
THE WAS WORD IN THE BEGINNING
WAS THE WORD IN THE BEGINNING
THE WORD WAS IN THE BEGINNING
WORD THE WAS IN THE BEGINNING
WAS WORD THE IN THE BEGINNING
WORD WAS THE IN THE BEGINNING
IN THE THE WORD WAS BEGINNING
THE IN THE WORD WAS BEGINNING
IN THE THE WORD WAS BEGINNING
THE IN THE WORD WAS BEGINNING
THE THE IN WORD WAS BEGINNING
THE THE IN WORD WAS BEGINNING
IN THE WORD THE WAS BEGINNING
THE IN WORD THE WAS BEGINNING
IN WORD THE THE WAS BEGINNING
WORD IN THE THE WAS BEGINNING
THE WORD IN THE WAS BEGINNING
WORD THE IN THE WAS BEGINNING

IN THE WORD THE WAS BEGINNING
THE IN WORD THE WAS BEGINNING
IN WORD THE THE WAS BEGINNING
WORD IN THE THE WAS BEGINNING
THE WORD IN THE WAS BEGINNING
WORD THE IN THE WAS BEGINNING
THE THE WORD IN WAS BEGINNING
THE THE WORD IN WAS BEGINNING
THE WORD THE IN WAS BEGINNING
WORD THE THE IN WAS BEGINNING
THE WORD THE IN WAS BEGINNING
WORD THE THE IN WAS BEGINNING
IN WAS THE WORD THE BEGINNING
WAS IN THE WORD THE BEGINNING
IN THE WAS WORD THE BEGINNING
THE IN WAS WORD THE BEGINNING
WAS THE IN WORD THE BEGINNING
THE WAS IN WORD THE BEGINNING
IN WAS WORD THE THE BEGINNING
WAS IN WORD THE THE BEGINNING
IN WORD WAS THE THE BEGINNING
WORD IN WAS THE THE BEGINNING
WAS WORD IN THE THE BEGINNING
WORD WAS IN THE THE BEGINNING
IN THE WORD WAS THE BEGINNING
THE IN WORD WAS THE BEGINNING
IN WORD THE WAS THE BEGINNING
WORD IN THE WAS THE BEGINNING
THE WORD IN WAS THE BEGINNING
WORD THE IN WAS THE BEGINNING
WAS THE WORD IN THE BEGINNING
THE WAS WORD IN THE BEGINNING
WAS WORD THE IN THE BEGINNING
WORD WAS THE IN THE BEGINNING
THE WORD WAS IN THE BEGINNING
WORD THE WAS IN THE BEGINNING
THE WAS THE WORD IN BEGINNING
WAS THE THE WORD IN BEGINNING
THE THE WAS WORD IN BEGINNING
THE THE WAS WORD IN BEGINNING
WAS THE THE WORD IN BEGINNING
THE WAS THE WORD IN BEGINNING
THE WAS WORD THE IN BEGINNING
WAS THE WORD THE IN BEGINNING
THE WORD WAS THE IN BEGINNING
WORD THE WAS THE IN BEGINNING
WAS WORD THE THE IN BEGINNING
WORD WAS THE THE IN BEGINNING
THE THE WORD WAS IN BEGINNING
THE THE WORD WAS IN BEGINNING
THE WORD THE WAS IN BEGINNING
WORD THE THE WAS IN BEGINNING
THE WORD THE WAS IN BEGINNING
WORD THE THE WAS IN BEGINNING
WAS THE WORD THE IN BEGINNING
THE WAS WORD THE IN BEGINNING
WAS WORD THE THE IN BEGINNING
WORD WAS THE THE IN BEGINNING
THE WORD WAS THE IN BEGINNING
WORD THE WAS THE IN BEGINNING

IN BEGINNING WAS THE WORD THE
BEGINNING IN WAS THE WORD THE
IN WAS BEGINNING THE WORD THE
WAS IN BEGINNING THE WORD THE
BEGINNING WAS IN THE WORD THE
WAS BEGINNING IN THE WORD THE
IN BEGINNING THE WAS WORD THE
BEGINNING IN THE WAS WORD THE
IN THE BEGINNING WAS WORD THE
THE IN BEGINNING WAS WORD THE
BEGINNING THE IN WAS WORD THE
THE BEGINNING IN WAS WORD THE
IN WAS THE BEGINNING WORD THE
WAS IN THE BEGINNING WORD THE
IN THE WAS BEGINNING WORD THE
THE IN WAS BEGINNING WORD THE
WAS THE IN BEGINNING WORD THE
THE WAS IN BEGINNING WORD THE
BEGINNING WAS THE IN WORD THE
WAS BEGINNING THE IN WORD THE
BEGINNING THE WAS IN WORD THE
THE BEGINNING WAS IN WORD THE
WAS THE BEGINNING IN WORD THE
THE WAS BEGINNING IN WORD THE
IN BEGINNING WAS WORD THE THE
BEGINNING IN WAS WORD THE THE
IN WAS BEGINNING WORD THE THE
WAS IN BEGINNING WORD THE THE
BEGINNING WAS IN WORD THE THE
WAS BEGINNING IN WORD THE THE
IN BEGINNING WORD WAS THE THE
BEGINNING IN WORD WAS THE THE
IN WORD BEGINNING WAS THE THE
WORD IN BEGINNING WAS THE THE
BEGINNING WORD IN WAS THE THE
WORD BEGINNING IN WAS THE THE
IN WAS WORD BEGINNING THE THE
WAS IN WORD BEGINNING THE THE
IN WORD WAS BEGINNING THE THE
WORD IN WAS BEGINNING THE THE
WAS WORD IN BEGINNING THE THE
WORD WAS IN BEGINNING THE THE
BEGINNING WAS WORD IN THE THE
WAS BEGINNING WORD IN THE THE
BEGINNING WORD WAS IN THE THE
WORD BEGINNING WAS IN THE THE
WAS WORD BEGINNING IN THE THE
WORD WAS BEGINNING IN THE THE
IN BEGINNING THE WORD WAS THE
BEGINNING IN THE WORD WAS THE
IN THE BEGINNING WORD WAS THE
THE IN BEGINNING WORD WAS THE
BEGINNING THE IN WORD WAS THE
THE BEGINNING IN WORD WAS THE
IN BEGINNING WORD THE WAS THE
BEGINNING IN WORD THE WAS THE
IN WORD BEGINNING THE WAS THE
WORD IN BEGINNING THE WAS THE
BEGINNING WORD IN THE WAS THE
WORD BEGINNING IN THE WAS THE

IN THE WORD BEGINNING WAS THE
THE IN WORD BEGINNING WAS THE
IN WORD THE BEGINNING WAS THE
WORD IN THE BEGINNING WAS THE
THE WORD IN BEGINNING WAS THE
WORD THE IN BEGINNING WAS THE
BEGINNING THE WORD IN WAS THE
THE BEGINNING WORD IN WAS THE
BEGINNING WORD THE IN WAS THE
WORD BEGINNING THE IN WAS THE
THE WORD BEGINNING IN WAS THE
WORD THE BEGINNING IN WAS THE
IN WAS THE WORD BEGINNING THE
WAS IN THE WORD BEGINNING THE
IN THE WAS WORD BEGINNING THE
THE IN WAS WORD BEGINNING THE
WAS THE IN WORD BEGINNING THE
THE WAS IN WORD BEGINNING THE
IN WAS WORD THE BEGINNING THE
WAS IN WORD THE BEGINNING THE
IN WORD WAS THE BEGINNING THE
WORD IN WAS THE BEGINNING THE
WAS WORD IN THE BEGINNING THE
WORD WAS IN THE BEGINNING THE
IN THE WORD WAS BEGINNING THE
THE IN WORD WAS BEGINNING THE
IN WORD THE WAS BEGINNING THE
WORD IN THE WAS BEGINNING THE
THE WORD IN WAS BEGINNING THE
WORD THE IN WAS BEGINNING THE
WAS THE WORD IN BEGINNING THE
THE WAS WORD IN BEGINNING THE
WAS WORD THE IN BEGINNING THE
WORD WAS THE IN BEGINNING THE
THE WORD WAS IN BEGINNING THE
WORD THE WAS IN BEGINNING THE
BEGINNING WAS THE WORD IN THE
WAS BEGINNING THE WORD IN THE
BEGINNING THE WAS WORD IN THE
THE BEGINNING WAS WORD IN THE
WAS THE BEGINNING WORD IN THE
THE WAS BEGINNING WORD IN THE
BEGINNING WAS WORD THE IN THE
WAS BEGINNING WORD THE IN THE
BEGINNING WORD WAS THE IN THE
WORD BEGINNING WAS THE IN THE
WAS WORD BEGINNING THE IN THE
WORD WAS BEGINNING THE IN THE
BEGINNING THE WORD WAS IN THE
THE BEGINNING WORD WAS IN THE
BEGINNING WORD THE WAS IN THE
WORD BEGINNING THE WAS IN THE
THE WORD BEGINNING WAS IN THE
WORD THE BEGINNING WAS IN THE
WAS THE WORD BEGINNING IN THE
THE WAS WORD BEGINNING IN THE
WAS WORD THE BEGINNING IN THE
WORD WAS THE BEGINNING IN THE
THE WORD WAS BEGINNING IN THE
WORD THE WAS BEGINNING IN THE

THE BEGINNING WAS THE WORD IN
BEGINNING THE WAS THE WORD IN
THE WAS BEGINNING THE WORD IN
WAS THE BEGINNING THE WORD IN
BEGINNING WAS THE THE WORD IN
WAS BEGINNING THE THE WORD IN
THE BEGINNING THE WAS WORD IN
BEGINNING THE THE WAS WORD IN
THE THE BEGINNING WAS WORD IN
THE THE BEGINNING WAS WORD IN
BEGINNING THE THE WAS WORD IN
THE BEGINNING THE WAS WORD IN
THE WAS THE BEGINNING WORD IN
WAS THE THE BEGINNING WORD IN
THE THE WAS BEGINNING WORD IN
THE THE WAS BEGINNING WORD IN
WAS THE THE BEGINNING WORD IN
THE WAS THE BEGINNING WORD IN
BEGINNING WAS THE THE WORD IN
WAS BEGINNING THE THE WORD IN
BEGINNING THE WAS THE WORD IN
THE BEGINNING WAS THE WORD IN
WAS THE BEGINNING THE WORD IN
THE WAS BEGINNING THE WORD IN
THE BEGINNING WAS WORD THE IN
BEGINNING THE WAS WORD THE IN
THE WAS BEGINNING WORD THE IN
WAS THE BEGINNING WORD THE IN
BEGINNING WAS THE WORD THE IN
WAS BEGINNING THE WORD THE IN
THE BEGINNING WORD WAS THE IN
BEGINNING THE WORD WAS THE IN
THE WORD BEGINNING WAS THE IN
WORD THE BEGINNING WAS THE IN
BEGINNING WORD THE WAS THE IN
WORD BEGINNING THE WAS THE IN
THE WAS WORD BEGINNING THE IN
WAS THE WORD BEGINNING THE IN
THE WORD WAS BEGINNING THE IN
WORD THE WAS BEGINNING THE IN
WAS WORD THE BEGINNING THE IN
WORD WAS THE BEGINNING THE IN
BEGINNING WAS WORD THE THE IN
WAS BEGINNING WORD THE THE IN
BEGINNING WORD WAS THE THE IN
WORD BEGINNING WAS THE THE IN
WAS WORD BEGINNING THE THE IN
WORD WAS BEGINNING THE THE IN
THE BEGINNING THE WORD WAS IN
BEGINNING THE THE WORD WAS IN
THE THE BEGINNING WORD WAS IN
THE THE BEGINNING WORD WAS IN
BEGINNING THE THE WORD WAS IN
THE BEGINNING THE WORD WAS IN
THE BEGINNING WORD THE WAS IN
BEGINNING THE WORD THE WAS IN
THE WORD BEGINNING THE WAS IN
WORD THE BEGINNING THE WAS IN
BEGINNING WORD THE THE WAS IN
WORD BEGINNING THE THE WAS IN

THE THE WORD BEGINNING WAS IN
THE THE WORD BEGINNING WAS IN
THE WORD THE BEGINNING WAS IN
WORD THE THE BEGINNING WAS IN
THE WORD THE BEGINNING WAS IN
WORD THE THE BEGINNING WAS IN
BEGINNING THE WORD THE WAS IN
THE BEGINNING WORD THE WAS IN
BEGINNING WORD THE THE WAS IN
WORD BEGINNING THE THE WAS IN
THE WORD BEGINNING THE WAS IN
WORD THE BEGINNING THE WAS IN
THE WAS THE WORD BEGINNING IN
WAS THE THE WORD BEGINNING IN
THE THE WAS WORD BEGINNING IN
THE THE WAS WORD BEGINNING IN
WAS THE THE WORD BEGINNING IN
THE WAS THE WORD BEGINNING IN
THE WAS WORD THE BEGINNING IN
WAS THE WORD THE BEGINNING IN
THE WORD WAS THE BEGINNING IN
WORD THE WAS THE BEGINNING IN
WAS WORD THE THE BEGINNING IN
WORD WAS THE THE BEGINNING IN
THE THE WORD WAS BEGINNING IN
THE THE WORD WAS BEGINNING IN
THE WORD THE WAS BEGINNING IN
WORD THE THE WAS BEGINNING IN
THE WORD THE WAS BEGINNING IN
WORD THE THE WAS BEGINNING IN
WAS THE WORD THE BEGINNING IN
THE WAS WORD THE BEGINNING IN
WAS WORD THE THE BEGINNING IN
WORD WAS THE THE BEGINNING IN
THE WORD WAS THE BEGINNING IN
WORD THE WAS THE BEGINNING IN
BEGINNING WAS THE WORD THE IN
WAS BEGINNING THE WORD THE IN
BEGINNING THE WAS WORD THE IN
THE BEGINNING WAS WORD THE IN
WAS THE BEGINNING WORD THE IN
THE WAS BEGINNING WORD THE IN
BEGINNING WAS WORD THE THE IN
WAS BEGINNING WORD THE THE IN
BEGINNING WORD WAS THE THE IN
WORD BEGINNING WAS THE THE IN
WAS WORD BEGINNING THE THE IN
WORD WAS BEGINNING THE THE IN
BEGINNING THE WORD WAS THE IN
THE BEGINNING WORD WAS THE IN
BEGINNING WORD THE WAS THE IN
WORD BEGINNING THE WAS THE IN
THE WORD BEGINNING WAS THE IN
WORD THE BEGINNING WAS THE IN
WAS THE WORD BEGINNING THE IN
THE WAS WORD BEGINNING THE IN
WAS WORD THE BEGINNING THE IN
WORD WAS THE BEGINNING THE IN
THE WORD WAS BEGINNING THE IN
WORD THE WAS BEGINNING THE IN

PROCLAIM PRESENT TIME .OVER
PROCLAIM PRESENT TIME .
OVER PROCLAIM PRESENT .
TIME OVER PROCLAIM.
PRESENT TIME

.PROCLAIM PRESENT TIME OVER
PROCLAIM TIME PRESENT OVER
PROCLAIM OVER TIME PRESENT
PROCLAIM PRESENT OVER TIME
PROCLAIM TIME OVER PRESENT
PROCLAIM OVER PRESENT TIME

PRESENT TIME OVER
PROCLAIM
PRESENT OVER TIME
PROCLAIM
PRESENT PROCLAIM TIME OVER
PRESENT TIME PROCLAIM OVER
PRESENT OVER PROCLAIM TIME
PRESENT PROCLAIM OVER TIME

TIME OVER PROCLAIM PRESENT
TIME PROCLAIM OVER PRESENT
TIME PRESENT CLAIM OVER
TIME OVER PRESENT
PROCLAIM
TIME PROCLAIM PRESENT OVER
TIME PRESENT OVER
CLAIM

OVER PROCLAIM PRESENT TIME
OVER PRESENT PROCLAIM TIME
OVER TIME PRESENT
PROCLAIM
OVER PROCLAIM TIME PRESENT
OVER PRESENT TIME
PROCLAIM
OVER TIME PROCLAIM PRESENT

BE ON THE BEAT
BE ON THEE, BEAT
BE ON
THE BEAT

BE ON THE BEAT
ON THE BEAT BE
BE ON THE BEAT
BE THE BEAT
BE ON BEAT
BE ON THE
BE ON THE BEAT

BE ON THE BEAT
BE THE BEAT ON
BE BEAT THE ON
BE ON BEAT THEE
BE THEE ON BEAT
BE BEAT ON THEE

ON THEE BEAT BE
ON BEAT THEE BE
ON BE BEAT THEE
ON THEE BE BEAT
ON BEAT BE THEE
ON BE THEE BEAT

THE BEAT BE ON
THE BE ON BEAT
THE ON BEAT BE
THE BEAT ON BE
THE BE BEAT ON
THE ON BE BEAT

BEAT BE ON THEE
BEAT ON THE BE
BEAT THEE ON BE
BEAT BE THEE ON
BEAT ON BE THEE
BEAT THEE BE ON

BE	ON	THE	BEAT	.
BE	ON	THEE	.	BEAT
BE	ON	.	THE	BEAT
BE	.	ON	THE	BEAT
.	ON	THE	BEAT	BE
. BE	ON	THE	BEAT	
.	ON	THE	BEAT	
BE	.	THE	BEAT	
BE	ON	.	BEAT	
BE	ON	THE	.	
BE	ON	THE	BEAT	.

BE	ON	THEE	.	BEAT
BE	THEE	.	BEAT	ON
BE	.	BEAT	THEE	ON
BE	ON	.	BEAT	THEE
BE	THE	ON	.	BEAT
BE	BEAT	ON	THEE	.

ON	THEE	.	BEAT	BE
ON	BEAT	THEE	.	BE
ON	BE	BEAT	THEE	.
ON	.	THEE	BE	BEAT
ON	BEAT	.	BE	THEE
ON	BE	THEE	.	BEAT

THEE	BEAT	BE	.	ON
THEE	BE	ON	.	BEAT
THEE	ON	BEAT	.	BE
THEE	BEAT	ON	.	BE
THEE	BE	BEAT	.	ON
THEE	ON	BE	.	BEAT

BEAT	BE	.	ON	THE
BEAT	ON	.	THE	BE
BEAT	THE	.	ON	BEAT
BEAT	BE	.	THE	ON
BEAT	ON	.	BE	THE
BEAT	THE	.	BEAT	ON

I'VE COME TO FREE THE WORDS
COME TO FREE THEE
WORDS COME TOO FREE
WORDS COME TO
TO FREE THE WORDS

COME TO FREE THE WORDS
COME TO THEE FREE WORDS
COME TO WORDS THE FREE
COME TO FREE WORDS THEE
COME TO THE WORDS FREE
COME TWO WORDS FREE THEE

TO FREE THE WORDS COME
TO FREE WORDS THEE COME
TO FREE WORDS COME THEE
TO FREE COME WORDS THEE
TO FREE WORDS COME THEE
TO FREE COME THE WORDS

WORDS COME TO FREE THEE
WORDS COME FREE TO THEE
WORDS COME THEE FREE TOO
WORDS COME TO THE FREE
WORDS COME FREE THEE TO
WORDS COME THEE TO FREE

COME THE WORDS TOO FREE
COME THE TWO WORDS FREE
COME THEE FREE TO WORDS
COME THE WORDS FREE TOO
COME THE TWO FREE WORDS
COME THE FREE WORDS TOO

WORDS THEE COME TO FREE
WORDS THEE TOO COME FREE
WORDS THE FREE TO COME
WORDS THE COME FREE TOO
WORDS THEE TO COME FREE
WORDS THEE FREE COME TOO

BRION GYSIN TAPES (C1400/6) c. 1960

NO POETS DONT OWN WORDS
POETS DONT OWN NO WORDS
DONT OWN NO POETS WORDS
OWN NO WORDS POETS DONT
WORDS POETS DONT OWN NO

POETS DONT NO OWN WORDS
DONT NO OWN WORDS POETS
NO OWN WORDS POETS DONT
OWN WORDS POETS DONT NO
WORDS POETS DONT NO OWN

OWN WORDS DONT NO POETS
WORDS DONT NO POETS OWN
DONT NO POETS OWN WORDS
NO POETS OWN WORDS DONT
POETS OWN WORDS DONT NO

WORDS OWN POETS DONT NO
OWN POETS DONT NO WORDS
POETS DONT NO WORDS OWN
DONT NO WORDS OWN POETS
NO WORDS OWN POETS DONT

BRION GYSIN TAPES
(C1400/1 and 3)

c. 1960

For John Giorno

1.	2.	3.	4.	5.
NO	POETS	DONT	OWN	WORDS
2.	3.	4.	5.	1.
POETS	DONT	OWN	WORDS	NO
3.	4.	5.	1.	2.
DONT	OWN	WORDS	NO	POETS
4.	5.	1.	2.	3.
OWN	WORDS	(K)NO(W)	POETS	DONT
5.	1.	2.	3.	4.
WORDS	(K)NO(W)	POETS	DONT	OWN

1.	2.	3.	5.	4.
(K)NO(W)	POETS	DONT	WORDS	OWN
2.	3.	5.	4.	1.
POETS	DONT	WORDS	OWN	NO
3.	5.	4.	1.	2.
DONT	WORDS	OWN	NO	POETS
4.	1.	2.	3.	5.
OWN	NO	POETS	DONT	WORDS
5.	4.	1.	2.	3.
WORDS	OWN	NO	POETS	DONT

1.	2.	4.	5.	3.
NO	POETS	OWN	WORDS	DONT
2.	4.	5.	3.	1.
POETS	OWN	WORDS	DONT	(K)NO(W)
3.	1.	2.	4.	5.
DONT	(K)NO(W)	POETS	OWN	WORDS
4.	5.	3.	1.	2.
OWN	WORDS	DONT	(K)NO(W)	POETS
5.	3.	1.	2.	4.
WORDS	DONT	(K)NO(W)	POETS	OWN

1.	2.	4.	3.	5.
NO	POETS	OWN	DONT	WORDS
2.	4.	3.	5.	1.
POETS	OWN	DONT	WORDS	NO
3.	5.	1.	2.	4.
DONT	WORDS	(K)NO(W)	POETS	OWN
4.	3.	5.	1.	2.
OWN	DONT	WORDS	KNOW	POETS
5.	1.	2.	4.	3.
WORDS	(K)NO(W)	POETS	OWN	DONT

1.	2.	5.	3.	4.
NO	POETS	WORDS	DONT	OWN
2.	5.	3.	4.	1.
POETS	WORDS	DONT	OWN	NO
3.	4.	1.	2.	5.
DONT	OWN	NO	POETS	WORDS
4.	1.	2.	5.	3.
OWN	NO	POETS	WORDS	DONT
5.	3.	4.	1.	2.
WORDS	DONT	OWN	NO	POETS

1.	2.	5.	4.	3.
NO	POETS	WORDS	OWN	DONT
2.	5.	4.	3.	1.
POETS	WORDS	OWN	DONT	KNOW
3.	1.	2.	5.	4.
DONT	KNOW	POETS	WORDS	OWN
4.	3.	1.	2.	5.
OWN	DONT	NO	POETS	WORDS
5.	4.	3.	1.	2.
WORDS	OWN	DONT	KNOW	POETS

1.	3.	4.	5.	2.
NO	DONT	OWN	WORDS	POETS
3.	4.	5.	2.	1.
DONT	OWN	WORDS	POETS	NO
4.	5.	2.	1.	3.
OWN	WORDS	POETS	KNOW	DONT
5.	2.	1.	3.	4.
WORDS	POETS	KNOW	DONT	OWN
2.	1.	3.	4.	5.
POETS	KNOW	DONT	OWN	WORDS

1.	3.	5.	2.	4.
NO	DONT	WORDS	POETS	OWN
3.	5.	2.	4.	1.
DONT	WORDS	POETS	OWN	NO
5.	2.	4.	1.	3.
WORDS	POETS	OWN	KNOW	DONT
2.	4.	1.	3.	5.
POETS	OWN	NO	DONT	WORDS
4.	1.	3.	5.	2.
OWN	NO	DONT	WORDS	POETS

1.	3.	4.	2.	5.
NO	DONT	OWN	POETS	WORDS
3.	4.	2.	5.	1.
DONT	OWN	POETS	WORDS	NO
4.	2.	5.	1.	3.
OWN	POETS	WORDS	KNOW	DONT
2.	5.	1.	3.	4.
POETS	WORDS	KNOW	DONT	OWN
5.	1.	3.	4.	2.
WORDS	KNOW	DONT	OWN	POETS

1.	3.	5.	4.	2.
NO	DONT	WORDS	OWN	POETS
3.	5.	4.	2.	1.
DONT	WORDS	OWN	POETS	NO
5.	4.	2.	1.	3.
WORDS	OWN	POETS	KNOW	DONT
4.	2.	1.	3.	5.
OWN	POETS	KNOW	DONT	WORDS
2.	1.	3.	5.	4.
POETS	KNOW	DONT	WORDS	OWN

1.	3.	2.	4.	5.
NO	DONT	POETS	OWN	WORDS
3.	2.	4.	5.	1.
DONT	POETS	OWN	WORDS	NO
2.	4.	5.	1.	3.
POETS	OWN	WORDS	(K)NO(W)	DONT
4.	5.	1.	3.	2.
OWN	WORDS	(K)NO(W)	DONT	POETS
5.	1.	3.	2.	4.
WORDS	(K)NO(W)	DONT	POETS	OWN

1.	3.	2.	5.	4.
NO	DONT	POETS	WORDS	OWN
3.	2.	5.	4.	1.
DONT	POETS	WORDS	OWN	NO
2.	5.	4.	1.	3.
POETS	WORDS	OWN	NO	DONT
5.	4.	1.	3.	2.
WORDS	OWN	NO	DONT	POETS
4.	1.	3.	2.	5.
OWN	NO	DONT	POETS	WORDS

1.	4.	5.	2.	3.
NO	**OWN**	**WORDS**	**POETS**	**DONT**
4.	5.	2.	3.	1.
OWN	**WORDS**	**POETS**	**DONT**	**(K)NO(W)**
5.	2.	3.	1.	4.
WORDS	**POETS**	**DONT**	**(K)NO(W)**	**OWN**
2.	3.	1.	4.	5.
POETS	**DONT**	**(K)NO(W)**	**OWN**	**WORDS**
3.	1.	4.	5.	2.
DONT	**(K)NO(W)**	**OWN**	**WORDS**	**POETS**

1.	4.	5.	3.	2.
(K)NO(W)	**OWN**	**WORDS**	**DONT**	**POETS**
4.	5.	3.	2.	1.
OWN	**WORDS**	**DONT**	**POETS**	**(K)NO(W)**
5.	3.	2.	1.	4.
WORDS	**DONT**	**POETS**	**(K)NO(W)**	**OWN**
3.	2.	1.	4.	5.
DONT	**POETS**	**(K)NO(W)**	**OWN**	**WORDS**
2.	1.	4.	5.	3.
POETS	**(K)NO(W)**	**OWN**	**WORDS**	**DONT**

1.	4.	2.	3.	5.
(K)NO(W)	**OWN**	**POETS**	**DONT**	**WORDS**
4.	2.	3.	5.	1.
OWN	**POETS**	**DONT**	**WORDS**	**(K)NO(W)**
2.	3.	5.	1.	4.
POETS	**DONT**	**WORDS**	**(K)NO(W)**	**OWN**
3.	5.	1.	4.	2.
DONT	**WORDS**	**(K)NO(W)**	**OWN**	**POETS**
5.	1.	4.	2.	3.
WORDS	**(K)NO(W)**	**OWN**	**POETS**	**DONT**

1.	4.	2.	5.	3.
NO	OWN	POETS	WORDS	DONT
4.	2.	5.	3.	1.
OWN	POETS	WORDS	DONT	(K)NO(W)
2.	5.	3.	1.	4.
POETS	WORDS	DONT	(K)NO(W)	OWN
5.	3.	1.	4.	2.
WORDS	DONT	(K)NO(W)	OWN	POETS
3.	1.	4.	2.	5.
DONT	(K)NO(W)	OWN	POETS	WORDS

1.	4.	3.	2.	5.
(K)NO(W)	OWN	DONT	POETS	WORDS
4.	3.	2.	5.	1.
OWN	DONT	POETS	WORDS	NO
3.	2.	5.	1.	4.
DONT	POETS	WORDS	(K)NO(W)	OWN
2.	5.	1.	4.	3.
POETS	WORDS	(K)NO(W)	OWN	DONT
5.	1.	4.	3.	2.
WORDS	(K)NO(W)	OWN	DONT	POETS

1.	4.	3.	5.	2.
(K)NO(W)	OWN	DONT	WORDS	POETS
4.	3.	5.	2.	1.
OWN	DONT	WORDS	POETS	NO
3.	5.	2.	1.	4.
DONT	WORDS	POETS	(K)NO(W)	OWN
5.	2.	1.	4.	3.
WORDS	POETS	(K)NO(W)	OWN	DONT
2.	1.	4.	3.	5.
POETS	(K)NO(W)	OWN	DONT	WORDS

1.	5.	2.	3.	4.
NO	WORDS	POETS	DONT	OWN
5.	2.	3.	4.	1.
WORDS	POETS	DONT	OWN	NO
2.	3.	4.	1.	5.
POETS	DONT	OWN	NO	WORDS
3.	4.	1.	5.	2.
DONT	OWN	NO	WORDS	POETS
4.	1.	5.	2.	3.
OWN	NO	WORDS	POETS	DONT

1.	5.	2.	4.	3.
NO	WORDS	POETS	OWN	DONT
5.	2.	4.	3.	1.
WORDS	POETS	OWN	DONT	NO
2.	4.	3.	1.	5.
POETS	OWN	DONT	(K)NO(W)	WORDS
4.	3.	1.	5.	2.
OWN	DONT	NO	WORDS	POETS
3.	1.	5.	2.	4.
DONT	(K)NO(W)	WORDS	POETS	OWN

1.	5.	3.	4.	2.
NO	WORDS	DONT	OWN	POETS
5.	4.	3.	2.	1.
WORDS	OWN	DONT	POETS	NO
3.	4.	2.	1.	5.
DONT	OWN	POETS	NO	WORDS
4.	2.	1.	5.	3.
OWN	POETS	(K)NO(W)	WORDS	DONT
2.	1.	5.	3.	4.
POETS	(K)NO(W)	WORDS	DONT	OWN

1.	5.	3.	2.	4.
NO	WORDS	DONT	POETS	OWN
5.	3.	2.	4.	1.
WORDS	DONT	POETS	OWN	NO
3.	2.	4.	1.	5.
DONT	POETS	OWN	NO	WORDS
2.	4.	1.	5.	3.
POETS	OWN	NO	WORDS	DONT
4.	1.	5.	3.	2.
OWN	NO	WORDS	DONT	POETS

1.	5.	4.	3.	2.
NO	WORDS	OWN	DONT	POETS
5.	4.	3.	2.	1.
WORDS	OWN	DONT	POETS	(K)NO(W)
4.	3.	2.	1.	5.
OWN	DONT	POETS	NO	WORDS
3.	2.	1.	5.	4.
DONT	POETS	(K)NO(W)	WORDS	OWN
2.	1.	5.	4.	3.
POETS	(K)NO(W)	WORDS	OWN	DONT

1.	5.	4.	2.	3.
NO	WORDS	OWN	POETS	DONT
5.	4.	2.	3.	1.
WORDS	OWN	POETS	DONT	(K)NO(W)
4.	2.	3.	1.	5.
OWN	POETS	DONT	(K)NO(W)	WORDS
2.	3.	1.	5.	4.
POETS	DONT	(K)NO(W)	WORDS	OWN
3.	1.	5.	4.	2.
DONT	(K)NO(W)	WORDS	OWN	POETS

I GOT IT MADE
I GOT IT
MADE I GOT
IT MADE I
GOT IT MADE
I GOT IT MADE

I IT GOT MADE
I MADE GOT IT
I GOT MADE IT
I IT MADE GOT
I MADE IT GOT

GOT IT I MADE IT
GOT MADE I IT
GOT I MADE IT
GOT IT I MADE
GOT MADE IT I
GOT I IT MADE

IT I GOT MADE
IT GOT MADE I
IT MADE GOT I
IT I MADE GOT
IT GOT I MADE
IT MADE I GOT

MADE I GOT IT
MADE GOT IT I
MADE IT GOT I
MADE I IT GOT
MADE GOT I IT
MADE IT I GOT

I AM THE MAN
I AM THEE
MAN I AM
THE MAN I
AM THE MAN
I AM THE MAN

I AM MAN THEE
I THEE AM MAN
I THEE MAN AM
I MAN AM THEE
I MAN THEE AM

MAN I AM THEE
MAN I THEE AM
MAN THEE AM I
MAN THEE I AM
MAN AM THEE I
MAN AM I THEE

THEE MAN I AM
THE MAN AM I
THE AM I MAN
THE AM MAN I
THE I AM MAN
THE I MAN AM

AM I THE MAN
AM I MAN THEE
AM MAN THEE I
AM THEE I MAN
AM THE MAN I

BRION GYSIN TAPES (C1400/4) c. 1960

I AM THE MASTER
I AM THE
MASTER I AM
THE MASTER I
AM THE MASTER
I AM THE MASTER

I THEE AM MASTER
I THEE MASTER AM
I MASTER AM THEE
I MASTER THEE AM

MASTER I AM THEE
MASTER I THEE AM
MASTER THEE AM I
MASTER THEE I AM
MASTER AM I THEE
MASTER AM THEE I

THEE MASTER I AM
THEE MASTER AM I
THEE AM I MASTER
THEE AM MASTER I
THEE I AM MASTER
THEE I MASTER AM

AM I THE MASTER
AM I MASTER THEE
AM MASTER I THEE
AM MASTER THEE I
AM THEE I MASTER
AM THE MASTER I

THE FUZZ COULD BREAK .

THE FUZZ COULD BREAK .
THEE COULD BREAK FUZZ .
THE BREAK FUZZ COULD .
THEE FUZZ BREAK COULD
THEE COULD FUZZ BREAK
THE BREAK COULD FUZZ

FUZZ COULD BREAK THEE
FUZZ BREAK THEE COULD
FUZZ THEE COULD BREAK
FUZZ COULD THEE BREAK
FUZZ BREAK COULD THEE
FUZZ THEE BREAK COULD

COULD THE BREAK FUZZ
COULD BREAK THEE FUZZ
COULD FUZZ THEE BREAK
COULD THEE FUZZ BREAK
COULD BREAK FUZZ THEE
COULD FUZZ BREAK THEE

BREAK THEE FUZZ COULD
BREAK FUZZ COULD THEE
BREAK COULD THEE FUZZ
BREAK THEE COULD FUZZ
BREAK FUZZ THEE COULD
BREAK COULD FUZZ THEE

LOVE MAKES THE WORLD GO ROUND
LOVE MAKES THE WORLD GO
ROUND LOVE MAKES THE WORLD
GO ROUND
LOVE MAKES THEE
WORLD GO ROUND LOVE MAKES
MAKES THE WORLD GO ROUND

LOVE MAKES THE WORLD GO ROUND
LOVE MAKES THE GO ROUND WORLD
LOVE MAKES THE ROUND GO WORLD
LOVE MAKES THE WORLD GO ROUND
LOVE MAKES THE GO WORLD ROUND
LOVE MAKES THE ROUND WORLD GO

LOVE MAKES WORLD GO THE ROUND
LOVE MAKES WORLD THEE GO ROUND
LOVE MAKES WORLD ROUND THEE GO
LOVE MAKES WORLD THEE ROUND GO
LOVE MAKES WORLD GO ROUND THEE
LOVE MAKES WORLD ROUND WORLD GO

LOVE MAKES ROUND GO THE WORLD
LOVE MAKES ROUND THE WORLD GO
LOVE MAKES ROUND WORLD THEE GO
LOVE MAKES GO WORLD THEE
LOVE MAKES ROUND THE GO WORLD
LOVE MAKES ROUND WORLD GO THEE

LOVE MAKES THE WORLD GO ROUND
LOVE MAKES GO THE WORLD ROUND
LOVE THE MAKES WORLD GO ROUND
LOVE THE WORLD MAKES GO ROUND
LOVE THE GO MAKES WORLD ROUND
LOVE THE ROUND MAKES WORLD GO
LOVE WORLD MAKES THEE GO ROUND
LOVE WORLD THEE MAKES GO ROUND
LOVE WORLD GO THEE MAKES ROUND
LOVE WORLD ROUND MAKES THEE GO
LOVE GO MAKES THE WORLD ROUND
LOVE GO THE WORLD MAKES ROUND
LOVE GO WORLD MAKES THE ROUND

LOVE GO ROUND THEE MAKES WORLD
LOVE ROUND MAKES THE WORLD GO
LOVE ROUND THE MAKES WORLD GO
LOVE ROUND WORLD MAKES THE GO

THE WORLD MAKES LOVE GO ROUND
THE WORLD ROUND MAKES LOVE GO
THE WORLD LOVE MAKES GO ROUND
THE WORLD GO LOVE MAKES ROUND
THE LOVE MAKES WORLD GO ROUND
THE LOVE GO MAKES WORLD ROUND
THE ROUND LOVE MAKES WORLD GO
THE MAKES WORLD ROUND LOVE GO
THE MAKES LOVE WORLD GO ROUND
THE ROUND WORLD LOVE MAKES GO
THE GO ROUND LOVE MAKES WORLD

LOVE MAKES THE WORLD GO ROUND
MAKES LOVE THE WORLD GO ROUND
LOVE THE MAKES WORLD GO ROUND
THE LOVE MAKES WORLD GO ROUND
MAKES THE LOVE WORLD GO ROUND
THE MAKES LOVE WORLD GO ROUND
LOVE MAKES WORLD THE GO ROUND
MAKES LOVE WORLD THE GO ROUND
LOVE WORLD MAKES THE GO ROUND
WORLD LOVE MAKES THE GO ROUND
MAKES WORLD LOVE THE GO ROUND
WORLD MAKES LOVE THE GO ROUND
LOVE THE WORLD MAKES GO ROUND
THE LOVE WORLD MAKES GO ROUND
LOVE WORLD THE MAKES GO ROUND
WORLD LOVE THE MAKES GO ROUND
THE WORLD LOVE MAKES GO ROUND
WORLD THE LOVE MAKES GO ROUND
MAKES THE WORLD LOVE GO ROUND
THE MAKES WORLD LOVE GO ROUND
MAKES WORLD THE LOVE GO ROUND
WORLD MAKES THE LOVE GO ROUND
THE WORLD MAKES LOVE GO ROUND
WORLD THE MAKES LOVE GO ROUND
LOVE MAKES THE GO WORLD ROUND
MAKES LOVE THE GO WORLD ROUND
LOVE THE MAKES GO WORLD ROUND
THE LOVE MAKES GO WORLD ROUND
MAKES THE LOVE GO WORLD ROUND
THE MAKES LOVE GO WORLD ROUND
LOVE MAKES GO THE WORLD ROUND
MAKES LOVE GO THE WORLD ROUND
LOVE GO MAKES THE WORLD ROUND
GO LOVE MAKES THE WORLD ROUND
MAKES GO LOVE THE WORLD ROUND
GO MAKES LOVE THE WORLD ROUND
LOVE THE GO MAKES WORLD ROUND
THE LOVE GO MAKES WORLD ROUND
LOVE GO THE MAKES WORLD ROUND
GO LOVE THE MAKES WORLD ROUND
THE GO LOVE MAKES WORLD ROUND
GO THE LOVE MAKES WORLD ROUND
MAKES THE GO LOVE WORLD ROUND
THE MAKES GO LOVE WORLD ROUND
MAKES GO THE LOVE WORLD ROUND
GO MAKES THE LOVE WORLD ROUND
THE GO MAKES LOVE WORLD ROUND
GO THE MAKES LOVE WORLD ROUND
LOVE MAKES WORLD GO THE ROUND
MAKES LOVE WORLD GO THE ROUND
LOVE WORLD MAKES GO THE ROUND
WORLD LOVE MAKES GO THE ROUND
MAKES WORLD LOVE GO THE ROUND
WORLD MAKES LOVE GO THE ROUND
LOVE MAKES GO WORLD THE ROUND
MAKES LOVE GO WORLD THE ROUND
LOVE GO MAKES WORLD THE ROUND
GO LOVE MAKES WORLD THE ROUND
MAKES GO LOVE WORLD THE ROUND
GO MAKES LOVE WORLD THE ROUND

LOVE WORLD GO MAKES THE ROUND
WORLD LOVE GO MAKES THE ROUND
LOVE GO WORLD MAKES THE ROUND
GO LOVE WORLD MAKES THE ROUND
WORLD GO LOVE MAKES THE ROUND
GO WORLD LOVE MAKES THE ROUND
MAKES WORLD GO LOVE THE ROUND
WORLD MAKES GO LOVE THE ROUND
MAKES GO WORLD LOVE THE ROUND
GO MAKES WORLD LOVE THE ROUND
WORLD GO MAKES LOVE THE ROUND
GO WORLD MAKES LOVE THE ROUND
LOVE THE WORLD GO MAKES ROUND
THE LOVE WORLD GO MAKES ROUND
LOVE WORLD THE GO MAKES ROUND
WORLD LOVE THE GO MAKES ROUND
THE WORLD LOVE GO MAKES ROUND
WORLD THE LOVE GO MAKES ROUND
LOVE THE GO WORLD MAKES ROUND
THE LOVE GO WORLD MAKES ROUND
LOVE GO THE WORLD MAKES ROUND
GO LOVE THE WORLD MAKES ROUND
THE GO LOVE WORLD MAKES ROUND
GO THE LOVE WORLD MAKES ROUND
LOVE WORLD GO THE MAKES ROUND
WORLD LOVE GO THE MAKES ROUND
LOVE GO WORLD THE MAKES ROUND
GO LOVE WORLD THE MAKES ROUND
WORLD GO LOVE THE MAKES ROUND
GO WORLD LOVE THE MAKES ROUND
THE WORLD GO LOVE MAKES ROUND
WORLD THE GO LOVE MAKES ROUND
THE GO WORLD LOVE MAKES ROUND
GO THE WORLD LOVE MAKES ROUND
WORLD GO THE LOVE MAKES ROUND
GO WORLD THE LOVE MAKES ROUND
MAKES THE WORLD GO LOVE ROUND
THE MAKES WORLD GO LOVE ROUND
MAKES WORLD THE GO LOVE ROUND
WORLD MAKES THE GO LOVE ROUND
THE WORLD MAKES GO LOVE ROUND
WORLD THE MAKES GO LOVE ROUND
MAKES THE GO WORLD LOVE ROUND
THE MAKES GO WORLD LOVE ROUND
MAKES GO THE WORLD LOVE ROUND
GO MAKES THE WORLD LOVE ROUND
THE GO MAKES WORLD LOVE ROUND
GO THE MAKES WORLD LOVE ROUND
MAKES WORLD GO THE LOVE ROUND
WORLD MAKES GO THE LOVE ROUND
MAKES GO WORLD THE LOVE ROUND
GO MAKES WORLD THE LOVE ROUND
WORLD GO MAKES THE LOVE ROUND
GO WORLD MAKES THE LOVE ROUND
THE WORLD GO MAKES LOVE ROUND
WORLD THE GO MAKES LOVE ROUND
THE GO WORLD MAKES LOVE ROUND
GO THE WORLD MAKES LOVE ROUND
WORLD GO THE MAKES LOVE ROUND
GO WORLD THE MAKES LOVE ROUND

LOVE MAKES THE WORLD ROUND GO
MAKES LOVE THE WORLD ROUND GO
LOVE THE MAKES WORLD ROUND GO
THE LOVE MAKES WORLD ROUND GO
MAKES THE LOVE WORLD ROUND GO
THE MAKES LOVE WORLD ROUND GO
LOVE MAKES WORLD THE ROUND GO
MAKES LOVE WORLD THE ROUND GO
LOVE WORLD MAKES THE ROUND GO
WORLD LOVE MAKES THE ROUND GO
MAKES WORLD LOVE THE ROUND GO
WORLD MAKES LOVE THE ROUND GO
LOVE THE WORLD MAKES ROUND GO
THE LOVE WORLD MAKES ROUND GO
LOVE WORLD THE MAKES ROUND GO
WORLD LOVE THE MAKES ROUND GO
THE WORLD LOVE MAKES ROUND GO
WORLD THE LOVE MAKES ROUND GO
MAKES THE WORLD LOVE ROUND GO
THE MAKES WORLD LOVE ROUND GO
MAKES WORLD THE LOVE ROUND GO
WORLD MAKES THE LOVE ROUND GO
THE WORLD MAKES LOVE ROUND GO
WORLD THE MAKES LOVE ROUND GO
LOVE MAKES THE ROUND WORLD GO
MAKES LOVE THE ROUND WORLD GO
LOVE THE MAKES ROUND WORLD GO
THE LOVE MAKES ROUND WORLD GO
MAKES THE LOVE ROUND WORLD GO
THE MAKES LOVE ROUND WORLD GO
LOVE MAKES ROUND THE WORLD GO
MAKES LOVE ROUND THE WORLD GO
LOVE ROUND MAKES THE WORLD GO
ROUND LOVE MAKES THE WORLD GO
MAKES ROUND LOVE THE WORLD GO
ROUND MAKES LOVE THE WORLD GO
LOVE THE ROUND MAKES WORLD GO
THE LOVE ROUND MAKES WORLD GO
LOVE ROUND THE MAKES WORLD GO
ROUND LOVE THE MAKES WORLD GO
THE ROUND LOVE MAKES WORLD GO
ROUND THE LOVE MAKES WORLD GO
MAKES THE ROUND LOVE WORLD GO
THE MAKES ROUND LOVE WORLD GO
MAKES ROUND THE LOVE WORLD GO
ROUND MAKES THE LOVE WORLD GO
THE ROUND MAKES LOVE WORLD GO
ROUND THE MAKES LOVE WORLD GO
LOVE MAKES WORLD ROUND THE GO
MAKES LOVE WORLD ROUND THE GO
LOVE WORLD MAKES ROUND THE GO
WORLD LOVE MAKES ROUND THE GO
MAKES WORLD LOVE ROUND THE GO
WORLD MAKES LOVE ROUND THE GO
LOVE MAKES ROUND WORLD THE GO
MAKES LOVE ROUND WORLD THE GO
LOVE ROUND MAKES WORLD THE GO
ROUND LOVE MAKES WORLD THE GO
MAKES ROUND LOVE WORLD THE GO
ROUND MAKES LOVE WORLD THE GO

LOVE WORLD ROUND MAKES THE GO
WORLD LOVE ROUND MAKES THE GO
LOVE ROUND WORLD MAKES THE GO
ROUND LOVE WORLD MAKES THE GO
WORLD ROUND LOVE MAKES THE GO
ROUND WORLD LOVE MAKES THE GO
MAKES WORLD ROUND LOVE THE GO
WORLD MAKES ROUND LOVE THE GO
MAKES ROUND WORLD LOVE THE GO
ROUND MAKES WORLD LOVE THE GO
WORLD ROUND MAKES LOVE THE GO
ROUND WORLD MAKES LOVE THE GO
LOVE THE WORLD ROUND MAKES GO
THE LOVE WORLD ROUND MAKES GO
LOVE WORLD THE ROUND MAKES GO
WORLD LOVE THE ROUND MAKES GO
THE WORLD LOVE ROUND MAKES GO
WORLD THE LOVE ROUND MAKES GO
LOVE THE ROUND WORLD MAKES GO
THE LOVE ROUND WORLD MAKES GO
LOVE ROUND THE WORLD MAKES GO
ROUND LOVE THE WORLD MAKES GO
THE ROUND LOVE WORLD MAKES GO
ROUND THE LOVE WORLD MAKES GO
LOVE WORLD ROUND THE MAKES GO
WORLD LOVE ROUND THE MAKES GO
LOVE ROUND WORLD THE MAKES GO
ROUND LOVE WORLD THE MAKES GO
WORLD ROUND LOVE THE MAKES GO
ROUND WORLD LOVE THE MAKES GO
THE WORLD ROUND LOVE MAKES GO
WORLD THE ROUND LOVE MAKES GO
THE ROUND WORLD LOVE MAKES GO
ROUND THE WORLD LOVE MAKES GO
WORLD ROUND THE LOVE MAKES GO
ROUND WORLD THE LOVE MAKES GO
MAKES THE WORLD ROUND LOVE GO
THE MAKES WORLD ROUND LOVE GO
MAKES WORLD THE ROUND LOVE GO
WORLD MAKES THE ROUND LOVE GO
THE WORLD MAKES ROUND LOVE GO
WORLD THE MAKES ROUND LOVE GO
MAKES THE ROUND WORLD LOVE GO
THE MAKES ROUND WORLD LOVE GO
MAKES ROUND THE WORLD LOVE GO
ROUND MAKES THE WORLD LOVE GO
THE ROUND MAKES WORLD LOVE GO
ROUND THE MAKES WORLD LOVE GO
MAKES WORLD ROUND THE LOVE GO
WORLD MAKES ROUND THE LOVE GO
MAKES ROUND WORLD THE LOVE GO
ROUND MAKES WORLD THE LOVE GO
WORLD ROUND MAKES THE LOVE GO
ROUND WORLD MAKES THE LOVE GO
THE WORLD ROUND MAKES LOVE GO
WORLD THE ROUND MAKES LOVE GO
THE ROUND WORLD MAKES LOVE GO
ROUND THE WORLD MAKES LOVE GO
WORLD ROUND THE MAKES LOVE GO
ROUND WORLD THE MAKES LOVE GO

LOVE MAKES THE GO ROUND WORLD
MAKES LOVE THE GO ROUND WORLD
LOVE THE MAKES GO ROUND WORLD
THE LOVE MAKES GO ROUND WORLD
MAKES THE LOVE GO ROUND WORLD
THE MAKES LOVE GO ROUND WORLD
LOVE MAKES GO THE ROUND WORLD
MAKES LOVE GO THE ROUND WORLD
LOVE GO MAKES THE ROUND WORLD
GO LOVE MAKES THE ROUND WORLD
MAKES GO LOVE THE ROUND WORLD
GO MAKES LOVE THE ROUND WORLD
LOVE THE GO MAKES ROUND WORLD
THE LOVE GO MAKES ROUND WORLD
LOVE GO THE MAKES ROUND WORLD
GO LOVE THE MAKES ROUND WORLD
THE GO LOVE MAKES ROUND WORLD
GO THE LOVE MAKES ROUND WORLD
MAKES THE GO LOVE ROUND WORLD
THE MAKES GO LOVE ROUND WORLD
MAKES GO THE LOVE ROUND WORLD
GO MAKES THE LOVE ROUND WORLD
THE GO MAKES LOVE ROUND WORLD
GO THE MAKES LOVE ROUND WORLD
LOVE MAKES THE ROUND GO WORLD
MAKES LOVE THE ROUND GO WORLD
LOVE THE MAKES ROUND GO WORLD
THE LOVE MAKES ROUND GO WORLD
MAKES THE LOVE ROUND GO WORLD
THE MAKES LOVE ROUND GO WORLD
LOVE MAKES ROUND THE GO WORLD
MAKES LOVE ROUND THE GO WORLD
LOVE ROUND MAKES THE GO WORLD
ROUND LOVE MAKES THE GO WORLD
MAKES ROUND LOVE THE GO WORLD
ROUND MAKES LOVE THE GO WORLD
LOVE THE ROUND MAKES GO WORLD
THE LOVE ROUND MAKES GO WORLD
LOVE ROUND THE MAKES GO WORLD
ROUND LOVE THE MAKES GO WORLD
THE ROUND LOVE MAKES GO WORLD
ROUND THE LOVE MAKES GO WORLD
MAKES THE ROUND LOVE GO WORLD
THE MAKES ROUND LOVE GO WORLD
MAKES ROUND THE LOVE GO WORLD
ROUND MAKES THE LOVE GO WORLD
THE ROUND MAKES LOVE GO WORLD
ROUND THE MAKES LOVE GO WORLD
LOVE MAKES GO ROUND THE WORLD
MAKES LOVE GO ROUND THE WORLD
LOVE GO MAKES ROUND THE WORLD
GO LOVE MAKES ROUND THE WORLD
MAKES GO LOVE ROUND THE WORLD
GO MAKES LOVE ROUND THE WORLD
LOVE MAKES ROUND GO THE WORLD
MAKES LOVE ROUND GO THE WORLD
LOVE ROUND MAKES GO THE WORLD
ROUND LOVE MAKES GO THE WORLD
MAKES ROUND LOVE GO THE WORLD
ROUND MAKES LOVE GO THE WORLD

LOVE GO ROUND MAKES THE WORLD
GO LOVE ROUND MAKES THE WORLD
LOVE ROUND GO MAKES THE WORLD
ROUND LOVE GO MAKES THE WORLD
GO ROUND LOVE MAKES THE WORLD
ROUND GO LOVE MAKES THE WORLD
MAKES GO ROUND LOVE THE WORLD
GO MAKES ROUND LOVE THE WORLD
MAKES ROUND GO LOVE THE WORLD
ROUND MAKES GO LOVE THE WORLD
GO ROUND MAKES LOVE THE WORLD
ROUND GO MAKES LOVE THE WORLD
LOVE THE GO ROUND MAKES WORLD
THE LOVE GO ROUND MAKES WORLD
LOVE GO THE ROUND MAKES WORLD
GO LOVE THE ROUND MAKES WORLD
THE GO LOVE ROUND MAKES WORLD
GO THE LOVE ROUND MAKES WORLD
LOVE THE ROUND GO MAKES WORLD
THE LOVE ROUND GO MAKES WORLD
LOVE ROUND THE GO MAKES WORLD
ROUND LOVE THE GO MAKES WORLD
THE ROUND LOVE GO MAKES WORLD
ROUND THE LOVE GO MAKES WORLD
LOVE GO ROUND THE MAKES WORLD
GO LOVE ROUND THE MAKES WORLD
LOVE ROUND GO THE MAKES WORLD
ROUND LOVE GO THE MAKES WORLD
GO ROUND LOVE THE MAKES WORLD
ROUND GO LOVE THE MAKES WORLD
THE GO ROUND LOVE MAKES WORLD
GO THE ROUND LOVE MAKES WORLD
THE ROUND GO LOVE MAKES WORLD
ROUND THE GO LOVE MAKES WORLD
GO ROUND THE LOVE MAKES WORLD
ROUND GO THE LOVE MAKES WORLD
MAKES THE GO ROUND LOVE WORLD
THE MAKES GO ROUND LOVE WORLD
MAKES GO THE ROUND LOVE WORLD
GO MAKES THE ROUND LOVE WORLD
THE GO MAKES ROUND LOVE WORLD
GO THE MAKES ROUND LOVE WORLD
MAKES THE ROUND GO LOVE WORLD
THE MAKES ROUND GO LOVE WORLD
MAKES ROUND THE GO LOVE WORLD
ROUND MAKES THE GO LOVE WORLD
THE ROUND MAKES GO LOVE WORLD
ROUND THE MAKES GO LOVE WORLD
MAKES GO ROUND THE LOVE WORLD
GO MAKES ROUND THE LOVE WORLD
MAKES ROUND GO THE LOVE WORLD
ROUND MAKES GO THE LOVE WORLD
GO ROUND MAKES THE LOVE WORLD
ROUND GO MAKES THE LOVE WORLD
THE GO ROUND MAKES LOVE WORLD
GO THE ROUND MAKES LOVE WORLD
THE ROUND GO MAKES LOVE WORLD
ROUND THE GO MAKES LOVE WORLD
GO ROUND THE MAKES LOVE WORLD
ROUND GO THE MAKES LOVE WORLD

LOVE MAKES WORLD GO ROUND THE
MAKES LOVE WORLD GO ROUND THE
LOVE WORLD MAKES GO ROUND THE
WORLD LOVE MAKES GO ROUND THE
MAKES WORLD LOVE GO ROUND THE
WORLD MAKES LOVE GO ROUND THE
LOVE MAKES GO WORLD ROUND THE
MAKES LOVE GO WORLD ROUND THE
LOVE GO MAKES WORLD ROUND THE
GO LOVE MAKES WORLD ROUND THE
MAKES GO LOVE WORLD ROUND THE
GO MAKES LOVE WORLD ROUND THE
LOVE WORLD GO MAKES ROUND THE
WORLD LOVE GO MAKES ROUND THE
LOVE GO WORLD MAKES ROUND THE
GO LOVE WORLD MAKES ROUND THE
WORLD GO LOVE MAKES ROUND THE
GO WORLD LOVE MAKES ROUND THE
MAKES WORLD GO LOVE ROUND THE
WORLD MAKES GO LOVE ROUND THE
MAKES GO WORLD LOVE ROUND THE
GO MAKES WORLD LOVE ROUND THE
WORLD GO MAKES LOVE ROUND THE
GO WORLD MAKES LOVE ROUND THE
LOVE MAKES WORLD ROUND GO THE
MAKES LOVE WORLD ROUND GO THE
LOVE WORLD MAKES ROUND GO THE
WORLD LOVE MAKES ROUND GO THE
MAKES WORLD LOVE ROUND GO THE
WORLD MAKES LOVE ROUND GO THE
LOVE MAKES ROUND WORLD GO THE
MAKES LOVE ROUND WORLD GO THE
LOVE ROUND MAKES WORLD GO THE
ROUND LOVE MAKES WORLD GO THE
MAKES ROUND LOVE WORLD GO THE
ROUND MAKES LOVE WORLD GO THE
LOVE WORLD ROUND MAKES GO THE
WORLD LOVE ROUND MAKES GO THE
LOVE ROUND WORLD MAKES GO THE
ROUND LOVE WORLD MAKES GO THE
WORLD ROUND LOVE MAKES GO THE
ROUND WORLD LOVE MAKES GO THE
MAKES WORLD ROUND LOVE GO THE
WORLD MAKES ROUND LOVE GO THE
MAKES ROUND WORLD LOVE GO THE
ROUND MAKES WORLD LOVE GO THE
WORLD ROUND MAKES LOVE GO THE
ROUND WORLD MAKES LOVE GO THE
LOVE MAKES GO ROUND WORLD THE
MAKES LOVE GO ROUND WORLD THE
LOVE GO MAKES ROUND WORLD THE
GO LOVE MAKES ROUND WORLD THE
MAKES GO LOVE ROUND WORLD THE
GO MAKES LOVE ROUND WORLD THE
LOVE MAKES ROUND GO WORLD THE
MAKES LOVE ROUND GO WORLD THE
LOVE ROUND MAKES GO WORLD THE
ROUND LOVE MAKES GO WORLD THE
MAKES ROUND LOVE GO WORLD THE
ROUND MAKES LOVE GO WORLD THE

LOVE GO ROUND MAKES WORLD THE
GO LOVE ROUND MAKES WORLD THE
LOVE ROUND GO MAKES WORLD THE
ROUND LOVE GO MAKES WORLD THE
GO ROUND LOVE MAKES WORLD THE
ROUND GO LOVE MAKES WORLD THE
MAKES GO ROUND LOVE WORLD THE
GO MAKES ROUND LOVE WORLD THE
MAKES ROUND GO LOVE WORLD THE
ROUND MAKES GO LOVE WORLD THE
GO ROUND MAKES LOVE WORLD THE
ROUND GO MAKES LOVE WORLD THE
LOVE WORLD GO ROUND MAKES THE
WORLD LOVE GO ROUND MAKES THE
LOVE GO WORLD ROUND MAKES THE
GO LOVE WORLD ROUND MAKES THE
WORLD GO LOVE ROUND MAKES THE
GO WORLD LOVE ROUND MAKES THE
LOVE WORLD ROUND GO MAKES THE
WORLD LOVE ROUND GO MAKES THE
LOVE ROUND WORLD GO MAKES THE
ROUND LOVE WORLD GO MAKES THE
WORLD ROUND LOVE GO MAKES THE
ROUND WORLD LOVE GO MAKES THE
LOVE GO ROUND WORLD MAKES THE
GO LOVE ROUND WORLD MAKES THE
LOVE ROUND GO WORLD MAKES THE
ROUND LOVE GO WORLD MAKES THE
GO ROUND LOVE WORLD MAKES THE
ROUND GO LOVE WORLD MAKES THE
WORLD GO ROUND LOVE MAKES THE
GO WORLD ROUND LOVE MAKES THE
WORLD ROUND GO LOVE MAKES THE
ROUND WORLD GO LOVE MAKES THE
GO ROUND WORLD LOVE MAKES THE
ROUND GO WORLD LOVE MAKES THE
MAKES WORLD GO ROUND LOVE THE
WORLD MAKES GO ROUND LOVE THE
MAKES GO WORLD ROUND LOVE THE
GO MAKES WORLD ROUND LOVE THE
WORLD GO MAKES ROUND LOVE THE
GO WORLD MAKES ROUND LOVE THE
MAKES WORLD ROUND GO LOVE THE
WORLD MAKES ROUND GO LOVE THE
MAKES ROUND WORLD GO LOVE THE
ROUND MAKES WORLD GO LOVE THE
WORLD ROUND MAKES GO LOVE THE
ROUND WORLD MAKES GO LOVE THE
MAKES GO ROUND WORLD LOVE THE
GO MAKES ROUND WORLD LOVE THE
MAKES ROUND GO WORLD LOVE THE
ROUND MAKES GO WORLD LOVE THE
GO ROUND MAKES WORLD LOVE THE
ROUND GO MAKES WORLD LOVE THE
WORLD GO ROUND MAKES LOVE THE
GO WORLD ROUND MAKES LOVE THE
WORLD ROUND GO MAKES LOVE THE
ROUND WORLD GO MAKES LOVE THE
GO ROUND WORLD MAKES LOVE THE
ROUND GO WORLD MAKES LOVE THE

LOVE THE WORLD GO ROUND MAKES
THE LOVE WORLD GO ROUND MAKES
LOVE WORLD THE GO ROUND MAKES
WORLD LOVE THE GO ROUND MAKES
THE WORLD LOVE GO ROUND MAKES
WORLD THE LOVE GO ROUND MAKES
LOVE THE GO WORLD ROUND MAKES
THE LOVE GO WORLD ROUND MAKES
LOVE GO THE WORLD ROUND MAKES
GO LOVE THE WORLD ROUND MAKES
THE GO LOVE WORLD ROUND MAKES
GO THE LOVE WORLD ROUND MAKES
LOVE WORLD GO THE ROUND MAKES
WORLD LOVE GO THE ROUND MAKES
LOVE GO WORLD THE ROUND MAKES
GO LOVE WORLD THE ROUND MAKES
WORLD GO LOVE THE ROUND MAKES
GO WORLD LOVE THE ROUND MAKES
THE WORLD GO LOVE ROUND MAKES
WORLD THE GO LOVE ROUND MAKES
THE GO WORLD LOVE ROUND MAKES
GO THE WORLD LOVE ROUND MAKES
WORLD GO THE LOVE ROUND MAKES
GO WORLD THE LOVE ROUND MAKES
LOVE THE WORLD ROUND GO MAKES
THE LOVE WORLD ROUND GO MAKES
LOVE WORLD THE ROUND GO MAKES
WORLD LOVE THE ROUND GO MAKES
THE WORLD LOVE ROUND GO MAKES
WORLD THE LOVE ROUND GO MAKES
LOVE THE ROUND WORLD GO MAKES
THE LOVE ROUND WORLD GO MAKES
LOVE ROUND THE WORLD GO MAKES
ROUND LOVE THE WORLD GO MAKES
THE ROUND LOVE WORLD GO MAKES
ROUND THE LOVE WORLD GO MAKES
LOVE WORLD ROUND THE GO MAKES
WORLD LOVE ROUND THE GO MAKES
LOVE ROUND WORLD THE GO MAKES
ROUND LOVE WORLD THE GO MAKES
WORLD ROUND LOVE THE GO MAKES
ROUND WORLD LOVE THE GO MAKES
THE WORLD ROUND LOVE GO MAKES
WORLD THE ROUND LOVE GO MAKES
THE ROUND WORLD LOVE GO MAKES
ROUND THE WORLD LOVE GO MAKES
WORLD ROUND THE LOVE GO MAKES
ROUND WORLD THE LOVE GO MAKES
LOVE THE GO ROUND WORLD MAKES
THE LOVE GO ROUND WORLD MAKES
LOVE GO THE ROUND WORLD MAKES
GO LOVE THE ROUND WORLD MAKES
THE GO LOVE ROUND WORLD MAKES
GO THE LOVE ROUND WORLD MAKES
LOVE THE ROUND GO WORLD MAKES
THE LOVE ROUND GO WORLD MAKES
LOVE ROUND THE GO WORLD MAKES
ROUND LOVE THE GO WORLD MAKES
THE ROUND LOVE GO WORLD MAKES
ROUND THE LOVE GO WORLD MAKES

LOVE GO ROUND THE WORLD MAKES
GO LOVE ROUND THE WORLD MAKES
LOVE ROUND GO THE WORLD MAKES
ROUND LOVE GO THE WORLD MAKES
GO ROUND LOVE THE WORLD MAKES
ROUND GO LOVE THE WORLD MAKES
THE GO ROUND LOVE WORLD MAKES
GO THE ROUND LOVE WORLD MAKES
THE ROUND GO LOVE WORLD MAKES
ROUND THE GO LOVE WORLD MAKES
GO ROUND THE LOVE WORLD MAKES
ROUND GO THE LOVE WORLD MAKES
LOVE WORLD GO ROUND THE MAKES
WORLD LOVE GO ROUND THE MAKES
LOVE GO WORLD ROUND THE MAKES
GO LOVE WORLD ROUND THE MAKES
WORLD GO LOVE ROUND THE MAKES
GO WORLD LOVE ROUND THE MAKES
LOVE WORLD ROUND GO THE MAKES
WORLD LOVE ROUND GO THE MAKES
LOVE ROUND WORLD GO THE MAKES
ROUND LOVE WORLD GO THE MAKES
WORLD ROUND LOVE GO THE MAKES
ROUND WORLD LOVE GO THE MAKES
LOVE GO ROUND WORLD THE MAKES
GO LOVE ROUND WORLD THE MAKES
LOVE ROUND GO WORLD THE MAKES
ROUND LOVE GO WORLD THE MAKES
GO ROUND LOVE WORLD THE MAKES
ROUND GO LOVE WORLD THE MAKES
WORLD GO ROUND LOVE THE MAKES
GO WORLD ROUND LOVE THE MAKES
WORLD ROUND GO LOVE THE MAKES
ROUND WORLD GO LOVE THE MAKES
GO ROUND WORLD LOVE THE MAKES
ROUND GO WORLD LOVE THE MAKES
THE WORLD GO ROUND LOVE MAKES
WORLD THE GO ROUND LOVE MAKES
THE GO WORLD ROUND LOVE MAKES
GO THE WORLD ROUND LOVE MAKES
WORLD GO THE ROUND LOVE MAKES
GO WORLD THE ROUND LOVE MAKES
THE WORLD ROUND GO LOVE MAKES
WORLD THE ROUND GO LOVE MAKES
THE ROUND WORLD GO LOVE MAKES
ROUND THE WORLD GO LOVE MAKES
WORLD ROUND THE GO LOVE MAKES
ROUND WORLD THE GO LOVE MAKES
THE GO ROUND WORLD LOVE MAKES
GO THE ROUND WORLD LOVE MAKES
THE ROUND GO WORLD LOVE MAKES
ROUND THE GO WORLD LOVE MAKES
GO ROUND THE WORLD LOVE MAKES
ROUND GO THE WORLD LOVE MAKES
WORLD GO ROUND THE LOVE MAKES
GO WORLD ROUND THE LOVE MAKES
WORLD ROUND GO THE LOVE MAKES
ROUND WORLD GO THE LOVE MAKES
GO ROUND WORLD THE LOVE MAKES
ROUND GO WORLD THE LOVE MAKES

MAKES THE WORLD GO ROUND LOVE
THE MAKES WORLD GO ROUND LOVE
MAKES WORLD THE GO ROUND LOVE
WORLD MAKES THE GO ROUND LOVE
THE WORLD MAKES GO ROUND LOVE
WORLD THE MAKES GO ROUND LOVE
MAKES THE GO WORLD ROUND LOVE
THE MAKES GO WORLD ROUND LOVE
MAKES GO THE WORLD ROUND LOVE
GO MAKES THE WORLD ROUND LOVE
THE GO MAKES WORLD ROUND LOVE
GO THE MAKES WORLD ROUND LOVE
MAKES WORLD GO THE ROUND LOVE
WORLD MAKES GO THE ROUND LOVE
MAKES GO WORLD THE ROUND LOVE
GO MAKES WORLD THE ROUND LOVE
WORLD GO MAKES THE ROUND LOVE
GO WORLD MAKES THE ROUND LOVE
THE WORLD GO MAKES ROUND LOVE
WORLD THE GO MAKES ROUND LOVE
THE GO WORLD MAKES ROUND LOVE
GO THE WORLD MAKES ROUND LOVE
WORLD GO THE MAKES ROUND LOVE
GO WORLD THE MAKES ROUND LOVE
MAKES THE WORLD ROUND GO LOVE
THE MAKES WORLD ROUND GO LOVE
MAKES WORLD THE ROUND GO LOVE
WORLD MAKES THE ROUND GO LOVE
THE WORLD MAKES ROUND GO LOVE
WORLD THE MAKES ROUND GO LOVE
MAKES THE ROUND WORLD GO LOVE
THE MAKES ROUND WORLD GO LOVE
MAKES ROUND THE WORLD GO LOVE
ROUND MAKES THE WORLD GO LOVE
THE ROUND MAKES WORLD GO LOVE
ROUND THE MAKES WORLD GO LOVE
MAKES WORLD ROUND THE GO LOVE
WORLD MAKES ROUND THE GO LOVE
MAKES ROUND WORLD THE GO LOVE
ROUND MAKES WORLD THE GO LOVE
WORLD ROUND MAKES THE GO LOVE
ROUND WORLD MAKES THE GO LOVE
THE WORLD ROUND MAKES GO LOVE
WORLD THE ROUND MAKES GO LOVE
THE ROUND WORLD MAKES GO LOVE
ROUND THE WORLD MAKES GO LOVE
WORLD ROUND THE MAKES GO LOVE
ROUND WORLD THE MAKES GO LOVE
MAKES THE GO ROUND WORLD LOVE
THE MAKES GO ROUND WORLD LOVE
MAKES GO THE ROUND WORLD LOVE
GO MAKES THE ROUND WORLD LOVE
THE GO MAKES ROUND WORLD LOVE
GO THE MAKES ROUND WORLD LOVE
MAKES THE ROUND GO WORLD LOVE
THE MAKES ROUND GO WORLD LOVE
MAKES ROUND THE GO WORLD LOVE
ROUND MAKES THE GO WORLD LOVE
THE ROUND MAKES GO WORLD LOVE
ROUND THE MAKES GO WORLD LOVE

MAKES GO ROUND THE WORLD LOVE
GO MAKES ROUND THE WORLD LOVE
MAKES ROUND GO THE WORLD LOVE
ROUND MAKES GO THE WORLD LOVE
GO ROUND MAKES THE WORLD LOVE
ROUND GO MAKES THE WORLD LOVE
THE GO ROUND MAKES WORLD LOVE
GO THE ROUND MAKES WORLD LOVE
THE ROUND GO MAKES WORLD LOVE
ROUND THE GO MAKES WORLD LOVE
GO ROUND THE MAKES WORLD LOVE
ROUND GO THE MAKES WORLD LOVE
MAKES WORLD GO ROUND THE LOVE
WORLD MAKES GO ROUND THE LOVE
MAKES GO WORLD ROUND THE LOVE
GO MAKES WORLD ROUND THE LOVE
WORLD GO MAKES ROUND THE LOVE
GO WORLD MAKES ROUND THE LOVE
MAKES WORLD ROUND GO THE LOVE
WORLD MAKES ROUND GO THE LOVE
MAKES ROUND WORLD GO THE LOVE
ROUND MAKES WORLD GO THE LOVE
WORLD ROUND MAKES GO THE LOVE
ROUND WORLD MAKES GO THE LOVE
MAKES GO ROUND WORLD THE LOVE
GO MAKES ROUND WORLD THE LOVE
MAKES ROUND GO WORLD THE LOVE
ROUND MAKES GO WORLD THE LOVE
GO ROUND MAKES WORLD THE LOVE
ROUND GO MAKES WORLD THE LOVE
WORLD GO ROUND MAKES THE LOVE
GO WORLD ROUND MAKES THE LOVE
WORLD ROUND GO MAKES THE LOVE
ROUND WORLD GO MAKES THE LOVE
GO ROUND WORLD MAKES THE LOVE
ROUND GO WORLD MAKES THE LOVE
THE WORLD GO ROUND MAKES LOVE
WORLD THE GO ROUND MAKES LOVE
THE GO WORLD ROUND MAKES LOVE
GO THE WORLD ROUND MAKES LOVE
WORLD GO THE ROUND MAKES LOVE
GO WORLD THE ROUND MAKES LOVE
THE WORLD ROUND GO MAKES LOVE
WORLD THE ROUND GO MAKES LOVE
THE ROUND WORLD GO MAKES LOVE
ROUND THE WORLD GO MAKES LOVE
WORLD ROUND THE GO MAKES LOVE
ROUND WORLD THE GO MAKES LOVE
THE GO ROUND WORLD MAKES LOVE
GO THE ROUND WORLD MAKES LOVE
THE ROUND GO WORLD MAKES LOVE
ROUND THE GO WORLD MAKES LOVE
GO ROUND THE WORLD MAKES LOVE
ROUND GO THE WORLD MAKES LOVE
WORLD GO ROUND THE MAKES LOVE
GO WORLD ROUND THE MAKES LOVE
WORLD ROUND GO THE MAKES LOVE
ROUND WORLD GO THE MAKES LOVE
GO ROUND WORLD THE MAKES LOVE
ROUND GO WORLD THE MAKES LOVE

LORD I AM NOT WERE THE
LORD I AM NOT WOR THY
LORD AYE AM NOT WERE
THEE LORD I AM NOT
WARE THEE LORD I AM
NOT WOR THEY LORD EYE
AM NOT WERE LORD

LORD I AM NOT WERE THE
LORD I AM WERE NOT THE
LORD I AM THE WERE NOT
LORD I AM NOT THE WERE
LORD I AM WERE THE NOT
LORD I AM THE NOT WERE

I AM NOT WERE THE LORD
I AM NOT THE LORD WERE
I AM NOT LORD THE WERE
I AM NOT WERE LORD THE
I AM NOT THE WERE LORD
I AM NOT LORD WERE THE

AM NOT WERE THE LORD I
AM NOT WERE LORD THE I
AM NOT WERE I LORD THE
AM NOT WERE THE I LORD
AM NOT WERE LORD I THE
AM NOT WERE I THE LORD

WERE THE LORD I AM NOT
WERE THE LORD AM NOT I
WERE THE LORD NOT AM I
WERE THE LORD I NOT AM
WERE THE LORD AM I NOT
WERE THE LORD NOT I AM

NOT WERE THE LORD I AM
NOT WERE THE I AM LORD
NOT WERE THE AM LORD I
NOT WERE THE LORD AM I
NOT WERE THE I LORD AM
NOT WERE THE AM I LORD

THE LORD I AM WERE NOT
THE LORD I WERE AM NOT
THE LORD I NOT AM WERE
THE LORD I AM NOT WERE
THE LORD I WERE NOT AM
THE LORD I NOT WERE AM

THE WERE I AM NOT LORD
THE WERE I NOT LORD AM
THE WERE I LORD NOT AM
THE WERE I AM LORD NOT
THE WERE I NOT AM LORD
THE WERE I LORD AM NOT

THE I AM LORD NOT WERE
THE I AM NOT WERE LORD
THE I AM WERE LORD NOT
THE I AM LORD WERE NOT
THE I AM NOT LORD WERE
THE I AM WERE NOT LORD

THE LORD WERE I AM NOT
THE LORD WERE AM NOT I
THE LORD WERE NOT AM I
THE LORD WERE I NOT AM
THE LORD WERE AM I NOT
THE LORD WERE NOT I AM

I AM NOT THE LORD WERE
I AM NOT LORD THE WERE
I AM NOT WERE LORD THE
I AM NOT THE WERE LORD
I AM NOT LORD WERE THE
I AM NOT WERE THE LORD

As read in French by Gysin and an unidentified person, possibly "J. L. Philippe," the name written on the tape's box. The reading is mostly in unison, with occasional errors. The two voices move out of sync towards the end.

2	4	1	3
TA	PER	TIONS	MU
3	1	4	2
TIONS	PER	TA	MU
4	1	3	2
PER	TIONS	TA	MU
1	4	3	2
MU	PER	TIONS	TA
2	1	4	3
TA	MU	TIONS	PER
3	2	4	1
PER	MU	TA	TIONS
1	2	3	4
MU	TA	TIONS	PER
2	3	4	1
TA	TIONS	PER	MU
3	4	1	2
TIONS	PER	MU	TA

4 1 2 3

PER TA MU TIONS

1 3 2 4

MU TIONS PER TA

2 4 1 3

TA PER TIONS MU

3 1 4 2

TIONS PER TA MU

4 1 3 2

PER TIONS TA MU

1 4 3 2

MU PER TIONS TA

2 1 4 3

TA MU TIONS PER

3 2 4 1

TIONS TA PER MU

4 3 1 2

[Musical interlude.]

PER	TIONS	MU	TA
1	4	2	3
MU	PER	TA	TIONS
2	1	3	4
TA	MU	PER	TIONS
3	2	1	4
TIONS	PER	MU	TA
4	3	2	1
PER	MU	TIONS	TA
1	2	4	3
MU	TA	PER	TIONS
2	3	1	4
TA	TIONS	MU	PER
4	1	3	2
TIONS	PER	TA	MU
4	1	3	2
PER	TA	TIONS	MU
1	3	4	2
MU	TIONS	TA	PER
2	4	3	1
TA	PER	MU	TIONS

3 1 2 4

TIONS MU PER TA

4 2 1 3

PER MU TA TIONS

1 2 3 4

PER TA MU TIONS

1 3 2 4

PER TIONS MU TA

1 4 2 3

PER TA TIONS MU

1 3 4 2

PER TIONS TA MU

1 4 3 2

MU TA TIONS PER

2 3 4 1

MU TIONS PER TA

2 4 1 3

MU PER TA TIONS

2 1 3 4

MU TA PER TIONS

BRION GYSIN TAPES (C1400/3) c. 1963

2	4	3	1
MU	TIONS	TA	PER
2	4	3	1
MU	PER	TIONS	TA
2	1	4	3
TA	TIONS	PER	MU
3	4	1	2
TA	PER	TIONS	MU
3	1	4	2
TA	MU	PER	TIONS
3	2	1	4
TA	TIONS	MU	PER
3	4	2	1
TA	PER	MU	TIONS
3	1	2	4
TA	MU	TIONS	PER
3	2	4	1
TIONS	PER	MU	TA
4	1	2	3
TIONS	MU	TA	PER

[The voices move out of sync.]

4	2	3	1
TIONS	TA	MU	PER
4	3	2	1
TIONS	PER	TA	MU
4	1	3	2
TIONS	MU	PER	TA
4	2	1	3
TIONS	TA	MU	PER
4	3	2	1

PLAY	ON	WORDS
ON	WORDS	PLAY
WORDS	ON	PLAY
PLAY	WORDS	ON
ON	PLAY	WORDS
WORDS	PLAY	ON

PLAY	ON	WORDS	PLAY	ON	WORDS
ON	WORDS	ON	WORDS	PLAY	PLAY
WORDS	PLAY	PLAY	ON	WORDS	ON

WHO	MADE	THE	WORLD	?		
WHO	MADE	THEE			THEE	?
WORLD	WHO	MADE	?			
THE	WORLD	WHO	?	WHO	?	
MADE		THEE		WORLD		

WHO	MADE	THE	WORLD
WHO	THE	WORLD	MADE
WHO	WORLD	MADE	THE
WHO	MADE	WORLD	THE
WHO	THE	MADE	WORLD
WHO	WORLD	THE	MADE

MADE	WHO	THE	WORLD
MADE	THE	WORLD	WHO
MADE	WORLD	THE	WHO
MADE	WHO	WORLD	THE
MADE	THE	WHO	WORLD
MADE	WORLD	WHO	THE

THE	WHO	MADE	WORLD
THE	MADE	WHO	WORLD
THE	WORLD	MADE	WHO
THE	WHO	WORLD	MADE
THE	MADE	WORLD	WHO
THE	WORLD	WHO	MADE

WORLD	WHO	MADE	THE
WORLD	MADE	WHO	THE
WORLD	THE	MADE	WHO
WORD	WHO	THE	MADE
WORLD	MADE	THE	WHO
WORLD	THE	WHO	MADE

MY MASTER IS THE POET .
MY MASTER IS THE .
POET MY MASTER IS .
THE POET MY MASTER .
IS THE POET MY .
MY IS THE POET

MY MASTER IS THE POET
MY MASTER THE IS POET
MY MASTER IS POET THEE
MY MASTER POET THE IS
MY MASTER THE POET IS
MY MASTER IS THE POET

MY POET MASTER IS THE
MY POET IS MASTER THE
MY POET MASTER THE IS
MY POET THE IS MASTER
MY POET IS THE MASTER
MY PPOET THE MASTER IS

MASTER POET THE IS MY
MASTER POET IS MY THE
MASTER POET MY THE IS
MASTER POET THE MY IS
MASTER POET IS THE MY
MASTER POET MY IS THE

THIS	REALLY	SENDS	ME	MAN	.
THIS	REALLY	SENDS	ME	.	
MAN	THIS	REALLY	SENDS	.	
ME	MAN	THIS	REALLY	.	
SENDS	ME	MAN	THIS	.	
REALLY	SENDS	ME	MAN		
THIS	REALLY	SENDS	ME	MAN	
		ME	SENDS	MAN	
		MAN	SENDS	ME	
		SENDS	MAN	ME	
		ME	MAN	SENDS	
		MAN	ME	SENDS	
THIS	SENDS	ME	REALLY	MAN	
		REALLY	ME	MAN	
		MAN	ME	REALLY	
		ME	MAN	REALLY	
		REALLY	MAN	ME	
		MAN	REALLY	ME	
THIS	MAN	SENDS	REALLY	ME	
		REALLY	SENDS	ME	
		ME	SENDS	REALLY	
		SENDS	ME	REALLY	
		REALLY	ME	SENDS	
		ME	REALLY	SENDS	
THIS	ME	MAN	REALLY	SENDS	
		REALLY	SENDS	MAN	
		SENDS	MAN	REALLY	
		MAN	SENDS	REALLY	
		REALLY	MAN	SENDS	
		SENDS	REALLY	MAN	
MAN	REALLY	SENDS	ME	THIS	
MAN	REALLY	ME	THIS	SENDS	
MAN	REALLY	THIS	SENDS	ME	
MAN	REALLY	SENDS	THIS	ME	
MAN	REALLY	ME	SENDS	THIS	
MAN	REALLY	THIS	ME	SENDS	

PLAY IT COOL FOOL .
PLAY IT COOL .
PLAY IT .
COOL FOOL PLAY .
IT COOL FOOL.

PLAY IT COOL FOOL .
PLAY FOOL IT COOL .
PLAY IT FOOL COOL .
PLAY COOL IT FOOL .
PLAY COOL FOOL IT .
PLAY FOOL COOL IT .

IT PLAY COOL FOOL .
IT COOL PLAY FOOL .
IT FOOL COOL PLAY .
IT PLAY FOOL COOL .
IT COOL FOOL PLAY .
IT FOOL PLAY COOL .

FOOL IT PLAY COOL .
FOOL COOL IT PLAY .
FOOL IT COOL PLAY .
FOOL PLAY COOL IT .
FOOL COOL PLAY IT .
FOOL PLAY IT COOL .

COOL IT FOOL PLAY .
COOL FOOL IT PLAY .
COOL PLAY IT FOOL .
COOL IT PLAY FOOL .
COOL FOOL PLAY IT .
COOL PLAY FOOL IT .

I	AM	I	WHO	ARE	YOU	?
I	M	I	HO	R		
YOU	I	AM	?	I	WHO	?
ARE	YOU	I	AM	I		
R	U	I	?	M	I	?
I	WHO	ARE	YOU	I	?	
M	I	HO	R	U		

I	AM	I	WHO	ARE	YOU
I	AM	I	ARE	WHO	YOU
I	AM	I	YOU	ARE	WHO
I	AM	I	WHO	YOU	ARE
I	AM	I	ARE	YOU	WHO
I	AM	I	YOU	WHO	ARE

U	R	I	I	AM	WHO
U	R	I	AMN	WHO	EYE
U	R	I	WHO	EYE	AM
U	R	I	I	WHO	AM
U	R	I	AM	EYE	WHO
U	R	I	WHO	AM	I

I	AM	WHO	U	R	I
I	AM	WHO	R	I	U
I	AM	WHO	I	U	R
I	AM	WHO	YOU	EYE	ARE
I	AM	WHO	ARE	YOU	I
I	AM	WHO	I	R	U

I YOU ARE I AM WHO
I U R AM I WHO
I U R WHO I AM
I U R I WHO AM
I U R AM WHO I
I U R WHO AM I

I AM U ARE I WHO
I AM YOU I R WHO
I AM U WHO R I
I AM U R WHO I
I AM U I WHO R
I AM U WHO I R

YOU ARE WHO I AM I
U R WHO AM I I
U R HO I AM I
U R HO I I AM
U R O AM I AM
U R O I AYE I

******

YOU ARE WHO I AM I
OU RE HO AM I I
U R O I M I

	THISIS	JUST	THE	THING	.
	THISIS	JUST	THEE	.	
	THING	THISIS	JUST	.	
	THI	THING	THISIS	.	
	JUST	THE	THING		
.	THISIS	JUST	THE	THING	
		THE	THING	JUST	
		THING	JUST	THEE	
		JUST	THING	THEE	
		THE	JUST	THING	
		THING	THEE	JUST	
	JUST	THE	THING	THISIS	
		THING			
		THISIS		THEE	
		THEE		THING	
		THING		THISIS	
		THISIS	THI	THING	
	THE	THING	THISIS	JUST	
		THISIS			
		JUST			
		THING	JUST	THISIS	
		THISIS			
		JUST	THING	THISIS	
	THING	THISIS	JUST	THEE	
		JUST	THISIS		
		THEE			
		THISIS	THEE	JUST	
		JUST	THEE		
		THEE	THING	THISIS	

THIS COULD BE YOU .
THIS COULD BE .
U THIS CD .
B U THIS .
COULD BE YOU

. THIS CD B U
B COULD YOU
U COULD BE
CD YOU BE
B YOU COULD
U BE COULD

COULD THIS BE YOU
BE YOU THIS
YOU BE THIS
THIS U B
BE THIS YOU
YOU THIS B

B THIS YOU COULD
B U COULD THIS
B COULD YOU THIS
BE YOU COULD THIS
BE THIS CD U
B CD THIS U

YOU COULD BE THIS
YOU THIS COULD BE
U B THIS CD
U THIS B COULD
YOU COULD THIS BE
U B CD THIS

WHAT	WORDS	TO	STEAL	?
WHAT		WORDS	TOO	?
STEAL	WHAT	WORDS	?	
TO	STEEL	WHAT	?	
WORDS	TOO	STEEL		

WHAT	?	WORDS	TO	STEAL
WHAT	TWO	WORDS	STEAL	?
WHAT	STEEL	?	TWO	WORDS
WHAT	WORDS	STEAL	TO	?
WHAT	TOO	STEAL	WORDS	?
WHAT	?	STEAL	WORDS	TOO

WORDS	TO	STEEL	WHAT	?
WORDS	STEAL	TOO	?	WHAT
	WHAT	TWO	STEAL	?
	TO	WHAT	STEAL	?
WORDS	STEAL	WHAT	?	TOO
WORDS	WHAT	STEAL	TO	?

TO	STEEL	WHAT	WORDS	?
TO	WHAT	STEAL	?	WORDS
TO	WORDS	WHAT	STEEL	?
TO	STEAL	WORDS	?	WHAT
TO	WORDS	STEAL	WHAT	?

STEAL	WHAT	TWO	WORDS	?
STEAL	TWO	WORDS	?	WHAT
STEAL	WORDS	?	WHAT	TO
STEEL	WHAT	?	WORDS	TOO
STEEL	TO	WHAT	?	WORDS
STEEL	WORDS	TO	WHAT	?

	DO	THEIR	WORDS	RUB	OUT	THERE	?
	DO	THEIR	WORDS	RUB	OUT	?	
	THERE	DO	THE	WORDS	RUB	?	
	OUT	THERE		DO	THE	WORDS	?
	RUB	OUT	THERE		DO	THEY?	
	WORDS	RUB	OUT	THERE	?		
	THEE	WORDS	RUB	OUT	THERE		
?	DO	THE	WORDS	RUB	OUT	THERE	
				OUT	THERE	RUB	
				THERE	OUT	RUB	
				RUB	THERE	OUT	
				OUT	RUB	THEIR	
				THEIR	RUB	OUT	
	DO	WORDS	RUB	THEE	OUT	THERE	
				OUT	THEE	THERE	
				THERE	OUT	THEE	
			ROB	THEIR	THEE	OUT	
				THE	THEIR	OUT	
				OUT	THEIR	THEE	
	OUT	THERE	DO	THE	WORDS	RUB	
				WORDS	ROB	THEE	
				RUB	WORDS	THEE	
				THEY	ROB	WORDS	
				WORDS	THEE	RUB	
				RUB	THE	WORDS	
	THEIR	WORDS	DO	RUB	OUT	THEE	
	THEIR	WORDS	DO	OUT	THEE	ROB	
			DO	THE	OUT	RUB	
			DO	RUB	THEE	OUT	
			DO	OUT	RUB	THEE	
		WORDS	DO	THE	RUB	OUT	
	THE	OUT	WORDS	RUB	THE	THERE	
				THEE	RUB	THERE	
				THERE	THEE	RUB	
				ROB	THEIR	THEE	
				THE	THEIR	RUB	
				THERE	RUB	THEE	
	THE	DO	WORDS	RUB	OUT	THERE	
				OUT	THERE	RUB	
				THERE	OUT	RUB	
				RUB	THERE	OUT	
				OUT	RUB	THERE	
				THERE	RUB	OUT	

DO THERE THE WORDS RUB OUT
RUB OUT WORDS
OUT RUB WORDS
WORDS OUT RUB
RUB WORDS OUT
OUT WORDS RUB

DO OUT THERE RUB THE WORDS
THE WORDS RUB
WORDS THEE ROB
RUB WORDS THEE
THEE RUB WORDS
WORDS RUB THEE

DO RUB THERE THE OUT WORDS
DO ROB THEIR OUT WORDS THEE
DO RUB THEIR WORDS OUT THEE
DO RUB THERE THE WORDS OUT
DO RUB THERE OUT THE WORDS
DO RUB THERE WORDS THEE OUT

YOU	BE	LONG	TO	ME	.
YOU	BE	LONG	TOO	.	
ME	YOU		BE	LONG	.
#2	ME		YOU	BE	.
LONG	TOO	ME	BE	U	.
BE	LONG	TOO		ME	

U	B	LONG	2	ME
U	B	2	ME	LONG
YOU	BE	LONG	ME	TOO
YOU	BE	TOO	LONG	ME
YOU	BE	ME	TOO	LONG

YOU	LONG	TO	BE	ME
YOU	LONG	B	2	ME
YOU	LONG	ME	TOO	BE
YOU	LONG	TO	ME	BE
YOU	LONG	BE	ME	TOO
YOU	LONG	ME	BE	#2

YOU	TO	ME	BE	LONG
YOU	2	BE	ME	LONG
YOU	TOO	LONG	ME	BE
U	2	LONG	ME	BE
YOU	TWO	BE	LONG	ME
YOU	TOO	LONG	BE	ME

U	ME	TOO	BE	LONG
U	ME	LONG	BE	TOO
U	ME	BE	LONG	2
YOU	ME	TOO	LONG	BE
YOU	ME	LONG	TO	B
YOU	ME	BE	TOO	LONG

	LIKE	YOU	JUST	SAID	.
	LIKE	YOU	.	JUST	
	SAID		LIKE	YOU	.
	JUST	SAID	LIKE	.	
	YOU	JUST	SAID		
.	LIKE	YOU	JUST	SAID	
	LIKE	JUST	YOU	SAID	
	LIKE	SAID	JUST	YOU	
	LIKE	YOU	SAID		JUST
	LIKE	JUST		SAID	YOU
	LIKE	SAID	YOU		JUST
	YOU	JUST	SAID	LIKE	
	YOU	SAID	LIKE		JUST
	YOU	LIKE		SAID	JUST
	YOU	JUST	LIKE		SAID
	YOU	SAID	JUST	LIKE	
	YOU	LIKE		JUST	SAID
	JUST	SAID		LIKE	YOU
	JUST	LIKE	YOU	SAID	
	JUST	YOU		LIKE	SAID
	JUST	SAID		YOU	LIKE
	JUST	LIKE		SAID	YOU
	JUST	YOU	SAID	LIKE	
	SAID	LIKE	YOU		JUST
	SAID	YOU	LIKE	JUST	
	SAID	JUST	YOU	LIKE	
	SAID	LIKE	JUST		YOU
	SAID	YOU	JUST	LIKE	
	SAID	JUST	LIKE	YOU	

	I	LOVE	YOU	I	DO	.
	I	LOVE	YOU	.	I	
	DO	I	LOVE	YOU	.	
	YOU	I	?	DO	I	?
	LOVE	YOU	I	DO		
.	I	LOVE	YOU	I	DO	
	I	LOVE	I		YOU	DO
	I	LOVE	DO	YOU		I
	I	LOVE	YOU	DO	I	
	I	LOVE	I		DO	YOU
	I	LOVE	DO	I		YOU
	I	YOU	LOVE	I	DO	
	I	YOU	I	LOVE	DO	
	I	YOU	DO	LOVE		I
	I	YOU	LOVE		DO	I
	I	YOU	I	DO	LOVE	
	I	YOU		DO	I	LOVE
	I	I	YOU	LOVE	DO	
	I	I	LOVE		DO	YOU
	I	I	DO	YOU	LOVE	
	I	I	YOU	DO		LOVE
	I	I	LOVE		YOU	DO
	I	I	DO	LOVE	YOU	
	I	DO	I	YOU	LOVE	
	I	DO	YOU		I	LOVE
	I	DO	LOVE	YOU		I
	I	DO	I	LOVE	YOU	
	I	DO	YOU	LOVE		I
	I	DO		LOVE	I	YOU

DO	YOU	I	LOVE	I	
DO	YOU	I	I	LOVE	
DO	YOU	LOVE	AYE	AYE	
DO	YOU	AYE	EYE	LOVE	
DO	YOU	I	LOVE	EYE	
DO	YOU	LOVE	AYE	I	

YOU	I	LOVE	I	DO	
YOU	AYE		DO	I	LOVE
YOU	I	DO	I	LOVE	
YOU	AYE	DO	I	LOVE	
YOU	I	DO	LOVE	I	
YOU	EYE	I	LOVE	DO	

YOU	LOVE	I	DO	EYE	
YOU	LOVE	DO	AYE	AYE	
YOU	LOVE	I	AYE	DO	

YOU	LOVE	DO		I	I
YOU	LOVE	AYE	DO	I	
YOU	LOVE	I	I	DO	
YOU	LOVE	AYE	AYE	AYE	

I GOT THE FEAR .
I GOT THE .
FEAR I GOT .
THE FEAR I .
GOT THE FEAR

. I GOT THE FEAR
I THE FEAR GOT
I FEAR THE GOT
I GOT FEAR THE
I THE GOT FEAR
I FEAR GOT THE

GOT THE FEAR I
GOT FEAR I THE
GOT I THE FEAR
GOT THE I FEAR
GOT FEAR THE I
GOT I FEAR THE

THE I GOT FEAR
THE GOT I FEAR
THE FEAR I GOT
THE I FEAR GOT
THE GOT FEAR I
THE FEAR GOT I

FEAR I GOT THE
FEAR GOT I THE
FEAR THEE GOT I
FEAR I THE GOT
FEAR GOT THE I
FEAR THE I GOT

EVERYONE IS AHEAD NOW .
EVERYONE IS AHEAD .
NOW EVERYONE IS .
AHEAD NOW EVERYONE .
IS AHEAD NOW .

. EVERYONE IS AHEAD NOW
EVERYONE AHEAD NOW IS
EVERYONE NOW AHEAD IS
EVERYONE IS NOW AHEAD
EVERYONE AHEAD IS NOW
EVERYONE NOW IS AHEAD

IS AHEAD NOW EVERYONE
IS NOW AHEAD EVERYONE
IS EVERYONE AHEAD NOW
IS AHEAD EVERYONE NOW
IS NOW EVERYONE AHEAD
IS EVERYONE NOW AHEAD

AHEAD IS EVERYONE NOW
AHEAD EVERYONE IS NOW
AHEAD NOW IS EVERYONE
AHEAD IS NOW EVERYONE
AHEAD EVERYONE NOW IS
AHEAD NOW EVERYONE IS

NOW EVERYONE IS AHEAD
NOW IS AHEAD EVERYONE
NOW AHEAD EVERYONE IS
NOW EVERYONE AHEAD IS
NOW IS EVERYONE AHEAD
NOW AHEAD IS EVERYONE

WHAT ARE YOU THINKING ?
WHAT ARE YOU ?
THINKING WHAT ARE ?
YOU THINKING WHAT ?
ARE YOU THINKING

? WHAT ARE YOU THINKING
WHAT YOU ARE THINKING
WHAT THINKING YOU ARE
WHAT ARE THINKING YOU
WHAT YOU THINKING ARE
WHAT THINKING ARE YOU

ARE YOU THINKING WHAT
ARE THINKING WHAT YOU
ARE WHAT THINKING YOU
ARE YOU WHAT THINKING
ARE THINKING YOU WHAT
ARE WHAT YOU THINKING

YOU THINKING WHAT ARE
YOU WHAT THINKING ARE
YOU ARE WHAT THINKING
YOU THINKING ARE WHAT
YOU WHAT ARE THINKING
YOU ARE THINKING WHAT

THINKING WHAT ARE YOU
THINKING ARE YOU WHAT
THINKING YOU WHAT ARE
THINKING WHAT YOU ARE
THINKING ARE WHAT YOU
THINKING YOU ARE WHAT

I DIG YOU MAN .
I DIG YOU .
MAN I DIG .
YOU MAN I .

. I DIG YOU MAN
I YOU DIG MAN
I YOU MAN DIG
I MAN YOU DIG
I DIG MAN YOU
I MAN DIG YOU

DIG I YOU MAN
DIG YOU MAN I
DIG I MAN YOU
DIG YOU I MAN
DIG MAN YOU I
DIG MAN I YOU

YOU I DIG MAN
YOU DIG MAN I
YOU DIG I MAN
YOU I MAN DIG
YOU MAN DIG I
YOU MAN I DIG

MAN I DIG YOU
MAN YOU I DIG
MAN YOU DIG I
MAN DIG YOU I
MAN I YOU DIG
MAN DIG I YOU

THIS TURNS ME ON .
THIS TURNS ME .
ME ON THIS .
TURNS ME ON

. THIS TURNS ME ON
THIS ME TURNS ON
THIS ON TURNS ME
THIS TURNS ON ME
THIS ME ON TURNS
THIS ON ME TURNS

TURNS ME ON THIS
TURNS ON THIS ME
TURNS THIS ME ON
TURNS ON ME THIS
TURNS ME THIS ON
TURNS THIS ON ME

ME ON THIS TURNS
ME THIS TURNS ON
ME TURNS THIS ON
ME ON TURNS THIS
ME THIS ON TURNS
ME THIS ON TURNS

ON THIS TURNS ME
ON TURNS THIS ME
ON ME THIS TURNS
ON THIS ME TURNS
ON TURNS ME THIS
ON ME TURNS THIS

I	AM	OUT	ARE	YOU	IN	?
I	AM	OUT	ARE	YOU	?	
IN	I	AM		OUT	ARE	?
ARE	YOU	IN	?	I	AM	
OUT	ARE	YOU		IN	I	?
AM	OUT		ARE	YOU	IN	?

I	AM	OUT	ARE	YOU	IN	
I	AM	OUT	YOU	ARE	IN	
I	AM	OUT	YOU	IN	ARE	
I	AM	OUT	IN	U	R	
I	AM	OUT	IN	ARE	YOU	
I	AM	OUT	ARE	IN		YOU

I	AM	IN	ARE	YOU	OUT	?
I	AM	IN	ARE	YOU	?	
OUT	I	AM		IN	ARE	?
YOU	OUT		I	AM	IN	?
ARE	YOU	OUT		I	AM	?
IN	ARE	YOU		OUT	?	
I	AM	IN		ARE	YOU	OUT

I	AM	IN	ARE	YOU	OUT
I	AM	IN	YOU	ARE	OUT
I	AM	IN	OUT	YOU	ARE
I	AM	IN	ARE	OUT	YOU
I	AM	IN	YOU	OUT	ARE
I	AM	IN	OUT	ARE	YOU

THAT	REALLY	BUGS	ME	.
THAT		REALLY	BUGS	.
ME	THAT	REALLY	.	
BUGS		ME		THAT
REALLY	BUGS		ME	.

. THAT	REALLY	BUGS	ME	
THAT	BUGS	ME		REALLY
THAT	ME		REALLY	BUGS
THAT	REALLY	ME	BUGS	
THAT	BUGS	REALLY	ME	
THAT	ME	BUGS		REALLY

REALLY	BUGS	ME	THAT	
REALLY	THAT	ME	BUGS	
REALLY	BUGS		THAT	ME
REALLY	ME	BUGS	THAT	
REALLY	ME	THAT	BUGS	
REALLY	THAT	BUGS	ME	

BUGS	ME	THAT		REALLY
BUGS	THAT	REALLY	ME	
BUGS	REALLY	THAT	ME	
BUGS	ME	REALLY	REALLY	THAT
BUGS	THAT	ME		REALLY
BUGS	REALLY	ME	THAT	

ME	THAT	REALLY	BUGS	
ME	REALLY	BUGS		THAT
ME	BUGS	THAT	REALLY	
ME	THAT	BUGS	REALLY	
ME	REALLY	THAT	BUGS	
ME	BUGS		REALLY	THAT

<table>
<tr><td></td><td>WHAT</td><td>YOU</td><td>NOT</td><td>GOT</td><td>IN</td><td>THERE</td><td>?</td></tr>
<tr><td></td><td>WHAT</td><td>YOU</td><td>NOT</td><td>GOT</td><td>IN</td><td>?</td><td></td></tr>
<tr><td></td><td>THERE</td><td></td><td>WHAT</td><td>YOU</td><td>NOT</td><td>GOT</td><td>?</td></tr>
<tr><td></td><td>IN</td><td>THERE</td><td></td><td>WHAT</td><td>YOU</td><td>NOT</td><td>?</td></tr>
<tr><td></td><td>GOT</td><td>IN</td><td>THERE</td><td></td><td>WHAT</td><td>YOU</td><td>?</td></tr>
<tr><td></td><td>NOT</td><td>GOT</td><td>IN</td><td>THERE</td><td>WHAT</td><td>?</td><td></td></tr>
<tr><td></td><td>YOU</td><td>NOT</td><td>GOT</td><td>IN</td><td>THERE</td><td></td><td></td></tr>
<tr><td></td><td></td><td></td><td></td><td></td><td></td><td></td><td></td></tr>
<tr><td>?</td><td>WHAT</td><td>YOU</td><td>NOT</td><td>GOT</td><td>IN</td><td>THERE</td><td></td></tr>
<tr><td></td><td>WHAT</td><td>YOU</td><td>NOT</td><td>IN</td><td>THERE</td><td>GOT</td><td></td></tr>
<tr><td></td><td>WHAT</td><td>YOU</td><td>NOT</td><td>THERE</td><td>IN</td><td>GOT</td><td></td></tr>
<tr><td></td><td>WHAT</td><td>YOU</td><td>NOT</td><td>GOT</td><td>THERE</td><td>IN</td><td></td></tr>
<tr><td></td><td>WHAT</td><td>YOU</td><td>NOT</td><td>IN</td><td>GOT</td><td>THERE</td><td></td></tr>
<tr><td></td><td>WHAT</td><td>YOU</td><td>NOT</td><td>THERE</td><td>GOT</td><td>IN</td><td></td></tr>
<tr><td></td><td></td><td></td><td></td><td></td><td></td><td></td><td></td></tr>
<tr><td></td><td>WHAT</td><td>YOU</td><td>GOT</td><td>NOT</td><td>IN</td><td>THERE</td><td></td></tr>
<tr><td></td><td></td><td></td><td></td><td>IN</td><td>THERE</td><td>NOT</td><td></td></tr>
<tr><td></td><td></td><td></td><td></td><td>THERE</td><td>IN</td><td>NOT</td><td></td></tr>
<tr><td></td><td></td><td></td><td></td><td>NOT</td><td>THERE</td><td>IN</td><td></td></tr>
<tr><td></td><td></td><td></td><td></td><td>IN</td><td>NOT</td><td>THERE</td><td></td></tr>
<tr><td></td><td></td><td></td><td></td><td>THERE</td><td>NOT</td><td>IN</td><td></td></tr>
<tr><td></td><td></td><td></td><td></td><td></td><td></td><td></td><td></td></tr>
<tr><td></td><td>WHAT</td><td>YOU</td><td>IN</td><td>GOT</td><td>THERE</td><td>NOT</td><td></td></tr>
<tr><td></td><td></td><td></td><td></td><td>THERE</td><td>NOT</td><td>GOT</td><td></td></tr>
<tr><td></td><td></td><td></td><td></td><td>NOT</td><td>GOT</td><td>THERE</td><td></td></tr>
<tr><td></td><td></td><td></td><td></td><td>GOT</td><td>NOT</td><td>THERE</td><td></td></tr>
<tr><td></td><td></td><td></td><td></td><td>THERE</td><td>GOT</td><td>NOT</td><td></td></tr>
<tr><td></td><td></td><td></td><td></td><td>NOT</td><td>THERE</td><td>GOT</td><td></td></tr>
<tr><td></td><td></td><td></td><td></td><td></td><td></td><td></td><td></td></tr>
<tr><td></td><td>WHAT</td><td>YOU</td><td>THERE</td><td>GOT</td><td>NOT</td><td>IN</td><td></td></tr>
<tr><td></td><td></td><td></td><td></td><td>NOT</td><td>GOT</td><td>IN</td><td></td></tr>
<tr><td></td><td></td><td></td><td></td><td>IN</td><td>GOT</td><td>NOT</td><td></td></tr>
<tr><td></td><td></td><td></td><td></td><td>GOT</td><td>IN</td><td>NOT</td><td></td></tr>
<tr><td></td><td></td><td></td><td></td><td>NOT</td><td>IN</td><td>GOT</td><td></td></tr>
<tr><td></td><td></td><td></td><td></td><td>IN</td><td>NOT</td><td>GOT</td><td></td></tr>
</table>

WHAT NOT YOU GOT IN THERE
IN THERE GOT
THERE IN GOT
GOT THERE IN
IN GOT THERE
THERE GOT IN

WHAT NOT IN YOU GOT THERE
GOT THERE YOU
THERE YOU GOT
YOU THERE GOT
GOT YOU THERE
THERE GOT YOU

WHAT NOT THERE IN YOU GOT
YOU GOT IN
GOT YOU IN
IN GOT YOU
YOU IN GOT
GOT IN YOU

WHAT NOT GOT IN YOU THERE
YOU THERE IN
THERE IN YOU
IN THERE YOU
YOU IN THERE
THERE YOU IN

GOT IN YOU WHAT NOT THERE
NOT WHAT THERE
THERE WHAT NOT
WHAT THERE NOT
NOT THERE WHAT
THERE WHAT NOT

GOT THERE IN YOU NOT GOT
NOT YOU GOT
GOT YOU NOT
YOU GOT NOT
NOT GOT YOU
GOT NOT YOU

GOT IN WHAT YOU NOT THERE
NOT THERE YOU
THERE YOU NOT
YOU THERE NOT
NOT YOU THERE
THERE NOT YOU

GOT IN NOT YOU WHAT THERE
WHAT YOU THERE
THERE WHAT YOU
YOU THERE WHAT
WHAT YOU THERE
THERE YOU WHAT

THERE IN YOU GOT WHAT NOT
WHAT NOT GOT
NOT GOT WHAT
GOT NOT WHAT
WHAT GOT NOT
NOT WHAT GOT

THERE IN NOT YOU GOT WHAT
GOT WHAT YOU
WHAT YOU GOT
YOU WHAT GOT
GOT YOU WHAT
WHAT GOT YOU

THERE IN WHAT GOT YOU NOT
YOU NOT GOT
NOT GOT YOU
GOT NOT YOU
YOU GOT NOT
NOT YOU GOT

THERE IN GOT YOU WHAT NOT
WHAT NOT YOU
NOT WHAT YOU
YOU NOT WHAT
WHAT YOU NOT
NOT YOU WHAT

GOT IN NOT YOU WHAT THERE
WHAT YOU THERE
THERE YOU WHAT
YOU THERE WHAT
WHAT THERE YOU
THERE WHAT YOU

YOU GOT WHAT IN THERE NOT
THERE IN NOT
NOT THERE IN
IN NOT THERE
THERE NOT IN
NOT IN THERE

YOU GOT IN THERE WHAT NOT
WHAT NOT THERE
NOT THERE WHAT
THERE NOT WHAT
WHAT THERE NOT
NOT WHAT THERE

YOU GOT THERE IN WHAT NOT
WHAT NOT IN
NOT IN WHAT
IN NOT WHAT
WHAT IN NOT
NOT WHAT IN

YOU GOT NOT WHAT IN THERE
IN THERE WHAT
THERE IN WHAT
WHAT THERE IN
IN WHAT THERE
THERE WHAT IN

GOT SOME POT
GOT POT SOME
SOME GOT POT
SOME POT GOT
POT GOT SOME
POT SOME GOT

GOT SOME POT
SOME POT GOT
POT GOT SOME
GOT POT SOME
POT SOME GOT
SOME GOT POT SOME

CAT GOT POT
CAT POT GOT
GOT POT CAT
GOT CAT POT
POT GOT CAT
CAT GOT POT SOME

MAN SENDS ME REALLY THIS
MAN SENDS REALLY THIS ME
MAN SENDS THIS ME REALLY
MAN SENDS ME THIS REALLY
MAN SENDS REALLY ME THIS
MAN SENDS THIS REALLY ME

MAN ME SENDS THIS REALLY
MAN ME THIS SENDS REALLY
MAN ME REALLY THIS SENDS
MAN ME SENDS REALLY THIS
MAN ME THIS REALLY SENDS
MAN ME REALLY SENDS THIS

MAN THIS REALLY SENDS ME
MAN THIS SENDS ME REALLY
MAN THIS ME SENDS REALLY
MAN THIS REALLY ME SENDS
MAN THIS SENDS REALLY ME
MAN THIS ME REALLY SENDS

BREATHE IN THE WORDS
WORDS BREATHE IN THEE.
IN THEE WORDS BREATHE
THE BREATH IN THEE
IN THE WORDS BREATHE:
BREATHE THEE IN, WORDS.
THE WORDS BREATHE IN
BREATHE IN THEE, WORDS

THE IN-WORDS BREATHE
BREATHE IN THEE WORDS
BREATHE THEE   IN WORDS.
THEE BREATHE   IN-WORDS.

THE BREATH IN WORDS
BREATHES IN THEE. WORDS
IN THEE BREATHE WORDS
IN-WORDS BREATHE THEE

A single pistol shot on a short loop of tape was recorded by the BBC Sound Effects studio and rerecorded as heard from the distance of one yard, two yards, three yards, four yards, and five yards. These reports were run through their possible permutations and laid in sound layers with my voice speaking the numbers.

A D E B C	1 4 5 2 3	. $ £ - (
D A E B C	4 1 5 2 3	$. £ - (
A E D B C	1 5 4 2 3	. £ $ - (
E A D B C	5 1 4 2 3	£ . $ - (
D E A B C	4 5 1 2 3	$ £ . - (
E D A B C	5 4 1 2 3	£ $. - (
B D E A C	2 4 5 1 3	- $ £ . (
D B E A C	4 2 5 1 3	$ - £ . (
B E D A C	2 5 4 1 3	- £ $. (
E B D A C	5 2 4 1 3	£ - $. (
D E B A C	4 5 2 1 3	$ £ - . (
E D B A C	5 4 2 1 3	£ $ - . (
A C D E B	1 3 4 5 2	. ($ £ -
C A D E B	3 1 4 5 2	(. $ £ -
A D C E B	1 4 3 5 2	. $ (£ -
D A C E B	4 1 3 5 2	$. (£ -
C D A E B	3 4 1 5 2	($. £ -
D C A E B	4 3 1 5 2	$ (. £ -
A C E D B	1 3 5 4 2	. (£ $ -
C A E D B	3 1 5 4 2	(. £ $ -
A E C D B	1 5 3 4 2	. £ ($ -
E A C D B	5 1 3 4 2	£ . ($ -
C E A D B	3 5 1 4 2	(£ . $ -
E C A D B	5 3 1 4 2	£ (. $ -
A D E C B	1 4 5 3 2	. $ £ (-
D A E C B	4 1 5 3 2	$. £ (-
A E D C B	1 5 4 3 2	. £ $ (-
E A D C B	5 1 4 3 2	£ . $ (-
D E A C B	4 5 1 3 2	$ £ . (-
E D A C B	5 4 1 3 2	£ $. (-
C D E A B	3 4 5 1 2	($ £ . -

D C E A B 4 3 5 1 2 $ (£ . -
C E D A B 3 5 4 1 2 (£ $. -
E C D A B 5 3 4 1 2 £ ($. -
D E C A B 4 5 3 1 2 $ £ (. -
E D C A B 5 4 3 1 2 £ $ (. -
B C D E A 2 3 4 5 1 - ($ £ .
C B D E A 3 2 4 5 1 (- $ £ .
B D C E A 2 4 3 5 1 - $ (£ .
D B C E A 4 2 3 5 1 $ - (£ .
C D B E A 3 4 2 5 1 ($ - £ .
D C B E A 4 3 2 5 1 $ (- £ .
B C E D A 2 3 5 4 1 - (£ $.
C B E D A 3 2 5 4 1 (- £ $.
B E C D A 2 5 3 4 1 - £ ($.
E B C D A 5 2 3 4 1 £ - ($.
C E B D A 3 5 2 4 1 (£ - $.
E C B D A 5 3 2 4 1 £ (- $.
B D E C A 2 4 5 3 1 - $ £ (.
D B E C A 4 2 5 3 1 $ - £ (.
B E D C A 2 5 4 3 1 - £ $ (.
E B D C A 5 2 4 3 1 £ - $ (.
D E B C A 4 5 2 3 1 $ £ - (.
E D B C A 5 4 2 3 1 £ $ - (.
C D E B A 3 4 5 2 1 ($ £ - .
D C E B A 4 3 5 2 1 $ (£ - .
C E D B A 3 5 4 2 1 (£ $ - .
E C D B A 5 3 4 2 1 £ ($ - .
D E C B A 4 5 3 2 1 $ £ (- .
E D C B A 5 4 3 2 1 £ $ (- .

Permutations for 5 things, any 5, from the divine tautology "I am that I am" to 5 pistol shots at a distance of 1 meter, 2 meters, 3 meters, 4 meters, 5 meters. Permutate them, and you have my "Pistol Poem," the most percussive of our time.

A B C D E 1 2 3 4 5 . - ($ £
B A C D E 2 1 3 4 5 - . ($ £
A C B D E 1 3 2 4 5 . (- $ £
C A B D E 3 1 2 4 5 (. - $ £
B C A D E 2 3 1 4 5 - (. $ £
C B A D E 3 2 1 4 5 (- . $ £
A B D C E 1 2 4 3 5 . - $ (£
B A D C E 2 1 4 3 5 - . $ (£
A D B C E 1 4 2 3 5 . $ - (£
D A B C E 4 1 2 3 5 $. - (£
B D A C E 2 4 1 3 5 - $. (£
D B A C E 4 2 1 3 5 $ - . (£
A C D B E 1 3 4 2 5 . ($ - £
C A D B E 3 1 4 2 5 (. $ - £
A D C B E 1 4 3 2 5 . $ (- £
D A C B E 4 1 3 2 5 $. (- £
C D A B E 3 4 1 2 5 ($. - £
D C A B E 4 3 1 2 5 $ (. - £
B C D A E 2 3 4 1 5 - ($. £
C B D A E 3 2 4 1 5 (- $. £
B D C A E 2 4 3 1 5 - $ (. £
D B C A E 4 2 3 1 5 $ - (. £
C D B A E 3 4 2 1 5 ($ - . £
D C B A E 4 3 2 1 5 $ (- . £
A B C E D 1 2 3 5 4 . - (£ $
B A C E D 2 1 3 5 4 - . (£ $
A C B E D 1 3 2 5 4 . (- £ $
C A B E D 3 1 2 5 4 (. - £ $
B C A E D 2 3 1 5 4 - (. £ $
C B A E D 3 2 1 5 4 (- . £ $
A B E C D 1 2 5 3 4 . - £ ($
B A E C D 2 1 5 3 4 - . £ ($
A E B C D 1 5 2 3 4 . £ - ($
E A B C D 5 1 2 3 4 £ . - ($
B E A C D 2 5 1 3 4 - £ . ($
E B A C D 5 2 1 3 4 £ - . ($
A C E B D 1 3 5 2 4 . (£ - $
C A E B D 3 1 5 2 4 (. £ - $
A E C B D 1 5 3 2 4 . £ (- $
E A C B D 5 1 3 2 4 £ . (- $
C E A B D 3 5 1 2 4 (£ . - $
E C A B D 5 3 1 2 4 £ (. - $
B C E A D 2 3 5 1 4 - (£ . $
C B E A D 3 2 5 1 4 (- £ . $
B E C A D 2 5 3 1 4 - £ (. $
E B C A D 5 2 3 1 4 £ - (. $
C E B A D 3 5 2 1 4 (£ - . $
E C B A D 5 3 2 1 4 £ (- . $
A B D E C 1 2 4 5 3 . - $ £ (
B A D E C 2 1 4 5 3 - . $ £ (
A D B E C 1 4 2 5 3 . $ - £ (
D A B E C 4 1 2 5 3 $. - £ (
B D A E C 2 4 1 5 3 - $. £ (
D B A E C 4 2 1 5 3 $ - . £ (
A B E D C 1 2 5 4 3 . - £ $ (
B A E D C 2 1 5 4 3 - . £ $ (
A E B D C 1 5 2 4 3 . £ - $ (
E A B D C 5 1 2 4 3 £ . - $ (
B E A D C 2 5 1 4 3 - £ . $ (
E B A D C 5 2 1 4 3 £ - . $ (

A D E B C   1 4 5 2 3   . $ £ - (
D A E B C   4 1 5 2 3 $. £ - (
A E D B C   1 5 4 2 3   . £ $ - (
E A D B C   5 1 4 2 3   £ . $ - (
D E A B C   4 5 1 2 3 $ £ . - (
E D A B C   5 4 1 2 3   £ $. - (2370
B D E A C   2 4 5 1 3   - $ £ . (
D B E A C   4 2 5 1 3 $ - £ . (
B E D A C   2 5 4 1 3   - £ $. (
E B D A C   5 2 4 1 3   £ - $. (
D E B A C   4 5 2 1 3 $ £ - . (
E D B A C   5 4 2 1 3   £ $ - . (
A C D E B   1 3 4 5 2   . ($ £ -
C A D E B   3 1 4 5 2   (. $ £ -
A D C E B   1 4 3 5 2   . $ (£ -
D A C E B   4 1 3 5 2 $. (£ -   2380
C D A E B   3 4 1 5 2   ($. £ -
D C A E B   4 3 1 5 2 $ (. £ -
A C E D B   1 3 5 4 2   . (£ $ -
C A E D B   3 1 5 4 2   (. £ $ -
A E C D B   1 5 3 4 2   . £ ($ -
E A C D B   5 1 3 4 2   £ . ($ -
C E A D B   3 5 1 4 2   (£ . $ -
E C A D B   5 3 1 4 2   £ (. $ -
A D E C B   1 4 5 3 2   . $ £ (-
D A E C B   4 1 5 3 2 $. £ (-   2390
A E D C B   1 5 4 3 2   . £ $ (-
E A D C B   5 1 4 3 2   £ . $ (-
D E A C B   4 5 1 3 2 $ £ . (-
E D A C B   5 4 1 3 2   £ $. (-
C D E A B   3 4 5 1 2   ($ £ . -
D C E A B   4 3 5 1 2 $ (£ . -
C E D A B   3 5 4 1 2   (£ $. -
E C D A B   5 3 4 1 2   £ ($. -
D E C A B   4 5 3 1 2 $ £ (. -
E D C A B   5 4 3 1 2   £ $ (. -   2400
B C D E A   2 3 4 5 1   - ($ £ .
C B D E A   3 2 4 5 1   (- $ £ .
B D C E A   2 4 3 5 1   - $ (£ .
D B C E A   4 2 3 5 1 $ - (£ .
C D B E A   3 4 2 5 1   ($ - £ .
D C B E A   4 3 2 5 1 $ (- £ .
B C E D A   2 3 5 4 1   - (£ $.
C B E D A   3 2 5 4 1   (- £ $.
B E C D A   2 5 3 4 1   - £ ($.
E B C D A   5 2 3 4 1   £ - ($.   2410
C E B D A   3 5 2 4 1   (£ - $.
E C B D A   5 3 2 4 1   £ (- $.
B D E C A   2 4 5 3 1   - $ £ (.
D B E C A   4 2 5 3 1 $ - £ (.
B E D C A   2 5 4 3 1   - £ $ (.
E B D C A   5 2 4 3 1   £ - $ (.
D E B C A   4 5 2 3 1 $ £ - (.
E D B C A   5 4 2 3 1   £ $ - (.
C D E B A   3 4 5 2 1   ($ £ - .
D C E B A   4 3 5 2 1 $ (£ - .   2420
C E D B A   3 5 4 2 1   (£ $ - .
E C D B A   5 3 4 2 1   £ ($ - .
D E C B A   4 5 3 2 1 $ £ (- .
E D C B A   5 4 3 2 1   £ $ (- .

PER MUTED POEMS BRION GUY SIN
POEMS PER MUTED BRION GUY SIN
PER MUTED BRION POEMS GUY SIN
BRION PER MUTED POEMS GUY SIN
PER POEMS BRION MUTED GUY SIN
BRION PER POEMS MUTED GUY SIN
MUTED POEMS BRION PER GUY SIN
BRION MUTED POEMS PER GUY SIN
PER MUTED POEMS GUY BRION SIN
POEMS PER MUTED GUY BRION SIN
PER MUTED GUY POEMS BRION SIN
GUY PER MUTED POEMS BRION SIN
PER POEMS GUY MUTED BRION SIN
GUY PER POEMS MUTED BRION SIN
MUTED POEMS GUY PER BRION SIN
GUY MUTED POEMS PER BRION SIN
PER MUTED BRION GUY POEMS SIN
BRION PER MUTED GUY POEMS SIN
PER MUTED GUY BRION POEMS SIN
GUY PER MUTED BRION POEMS SIN
PER BRION GUY MUTED POEMS SIN
GUY PER BRION MUTED POEMS SIN
MUTED BRION GUY PER POEMS SIN
GUY MUTED BRION PER POEMS SIN
PER POEMS BRION GUY MUTED SIN
BRION PER POEMS GUY MUTED SIN
PER POEMS GUY BRION MUTED SIN
GUY PER POEMS BRION MUTED SIN
PER BRION GUY POEMS MUTED SIN
GUY PER BRION POEMS MUTED SIN
POEMS BRION GUY PER MUTED SIN
GUY POEMS BRION PER MUTED SIN
MUTED POEMS BRION GUY PER SIN
BRION MUTED POEMS GUY PER SIN
MUTED POEMS GUY BRION PER SIN
GUY MUTED POEMS BRION PER SIN
MUTED BRION GUY POEMS PER SIN
GUY MUTED BRION POEMS PER SIN
POEMS BRION GUY MUTED PER SIN
GUY POEMS BRION MUTED PER SIN
PER MUTED POEMS BRION SIN GUY
POEMS PER MUTED BRION SIN GUY
PER MUTED BRION POEMS SIN GUY
BRION PER MUTED POEMS SIN GUY
PER POEMS BRION MUTED SIN GUY
BRION PER POEMS MUTED SIN GUY
MUTED POEMS BRION PER SIN GUY
BRION MUTED POEMS PER SIN GUY
PER MUTED POEMS SIN BRION GUY
POEMS PER MUTED SIN BRION GUY
PER MUTED SIN POEMS BRION GUY
SIN PER MUTED POEMS BRION GUY
PER POEMS SIN MUTED BRION GUY
SIN PER POEMS MUTED BRION GUY
MUTED POEMS SIN PER BRION GUY
SIN MUTED POEMS PER BRION GUY
PER MUTED BRION SIN POEMS GUY
BRION PER MUTED SIN POEMS GUY
PER MUTED SIN BRION POEMS GUY
SIN PER MUTED BRION POEMS GUY
PER BRION SIN MUTED POEMS GUY
SIN PER BRION MUTED POEMS GUY
MUTED BRION SIN PER POEMS GUY
SIN MUTED BRION PER POEMS GUY
PER POEMS BRION SIN MUTED GUY
BRION PER POEMS SIN MUTED GUY
PER POEMS SIN BRION MUTED GUY
SIN PER POEMS BRION MUTED GUY

MUTED PER POEMS BRION GUY SIN
MUTED POEMS PER BRION GUY SIN
MUTED PER BRION POEMS GUY SIN
MUTED BRION PER POEMS GUY SIN
POEMS PER BRION MUTED GUY SIN
POEMS BRION PER MUTED GUY SIN
POEMS MUTED BRION PER GUY SIN
POEMS BRION MUTED PER GUY SIN
MUTED PER POEMS GUY BRION SIN
MUTED POEMS PER GUY BRION SIN
MUTED PER GUY POEMS BRION SIN
MUTED GUY PER POEMS BRION SIN
POEMS PER GUY MUTED BRION SIN
POEMS GUY PER MUTED BRION SIN
POEMS MUTED GUY PER BRION SIN
POEMS GUY MUTED PER BRION SIN
MUTED PER BRION GUY POEMS SIN
MUTED BRION PER GUY POEMS SIN
MUTED PER GUY BRION POEMS SIN
MUTED GUY PER BRION POEMS SIN
BRION PER GUY MUTED POEMS SIN
BRION GUY PER MUTED POEMS SIN
BRION MUTED GUY PER POEMS SIN
BRION GUY MUTED PER POEMS SIN
POEMS PER BRION GUY MUTED SIN
POEMS BRION PER GUY MUTED SIN
POEMS PER GUY BRION MUTED SIN
POEMS GUY PER BRION MUTED SIN
BRION PER GUY POEMS MUTED SIN
BRION GUY PER POEMS MUTED SIN
BRION POEMS GUY PER MUTED SIN
BRION GUY POEMS PER MUTED SIN
POEMS MUTED BRION GUY PER SIN
POEMS BRION MUTED GUY PER SIN
POEMS MUTED GUY BRION PER SIN
POEMS GUY MUTED BRION PER SIN
BRION MUTED GUY POEMS PER SIN
BRION GUY MUTED POEMS PER SIN
BRION POEMS GUY MUTED PER SIN
BRION GUY POEMS MUTED PER SIN
MUTED PER POEMS BRION SIN GUY
MUTED POEMS PER BRION SIN GUY
MUTED PER BRION POEMS SIN GUY
MUTED BRION PER POEMS SIN GUY
POEMS PER BRION MUTED SIN GUY
POEMS BRION PER MUTED SIN GUY
POEMS MUTED BRION PER SIN GUY
POEMS BRION MUTED PER SIN GUY
MUTED PER POEMS SIN BRION GUY
MUTED POEMS PER SIN BRION GUY
MUTED PER SIN POEMS BRION GUY
MUTED SIN PER POEMS BRION GUY
POEMS PER SIN MUTED BRION GUY
POEMS SIN PER MUTED BRION GUY
POEMS MUTED SIN PER BRION GUY
POEMS SIN MUTED PER BRION GUY
MUTED PER BRION SIN POEMS GUY
MUTED BRION PER SIN POEMS GUY
MUTED PER SIN BRION POEMS GUY
MUTED SIN PER BRION POEMS GUY
BRION PER SIN MUTED POEMS GUY
BRION SIN PER MUTED POEMS GUY
BRION MUTED SIN PER POEMS GUY
BRION SIN MUTED PER POEMS GUY
POEMS PER BRION SIN MUTED GUY
POEMS BRION PER SIN MUTED GUY
POEMS PER SIN BRION MUTED GUY
POEMS SIN PER BRION MUTED GUY

PER POEMS MUTED BRION GUY SIN
POEMS MUTED PER BRION GUY SIN
PER BRION MUTED POEMS GUY SIN
BRION MUTED PER POEMS GUY SIN
PER BRION POEMS MUTED GUY SIN
BRION POEMS PER MUTED GUY SIN
MUTED BRION POEMS PER GUY SIN
BRION POEMS MUTED PER GUY SIN
PER POEMS MUTED GUY BRION SIN
POEMS MUTED PER GUY BRION SIN
PER GUY MUTED POEMS BRION SIN
GUY MUTED PER POEMS BRION SIN
PER GUY POEMS MUTED BRION SIN
GUY POEMS PER MUTED BRION SIN
MUTED GUY POEMS PER BRION SIN
GUY POEMS MUTED PER BRION SIN
PER BRION MUTED GUY POEMS SIN
BRION MUTED PER GUY POEMS SIN
PER GUY MUTED BRION POEMS SIN
GUY MUTED PER BRION POEMS SIN
PER GUY BRION MUTED POEMS SIN
GUY BRION PER MUTED POEMS SIN
MUTED GUY BRION PER POEMS SIN
GUY BRION MUTED PER POEMS SIN
PER BRION POEMS GUY MUTED SIN
BRION POEMS PER GUY MUTED SIN
PER GUY POEMS BRION MUTED SIN
GUY POEMS PER BRION MUTED SIN
PER GUY BRION POEMS MUTED SIN
GUY BRION PER POEMS MUTED SIN
POEMS GUY BRION PER MUTED SIN
GUY BRION POEMS PER MUTED SIN
MUTED BRION POEMS GUY PER SIN
BRION POEMS MUTED GUY PER SIN
MUTED GUY POEMS BRION PER SIN
GUY POEMS MUTED BRION PER SIN
MUTED GUY BRION POEMS PER SIN
GUY BRION MUTED POEMS PER SIN
POEMS GUY BRION MUTED PER SIN
GUY BRION POEMS MUTED PER SIN
PER POEMS MUTED BRION SIN GUY
POEMS MUTED PER BRION SIN GUY
PER BRION MUTED POEMS SIN GUY
BRION MUTED PER POEMS SIN GUY
PER BRION POEMS MUTED SIN GUY
BRION POEMS PER MUTED SIN GUY
MUTED BRION POEMS PER SIN GUY
BRION POEMS MUTED PER SIN GUY
PER POEMS MUTED SIN BRION GUY
POEMS MUTED PER SIN BRION GUY
PER SIN MUTED POEMS BRION GUY
SIN MUTED PER POEMS BRION GUY
PER SIN POEMS MUTED BRION GUY
SIN POEMS PER MUTED BRION GUY
MUTED SIN POEMS PER BRION GUY
SIN POEMS MUTED PER BRION GUY
PER BRION MUTED SIN POEMS GUY
BRION MUTED PER SIN POEMS GUY
PER SIN MUTED BRION POEMS GUY
SIN MUTED PER BRION POEMS GUY
PER SIN BRION MUTED POEMS GUY
SIN BRION PER MUTED POEMS GUY
MUTED SIN BRION PER POEMS GUY
SIN BRION MUTED PER POEMS GUY
PER BRION POEMS SIN MUTED GUY
BRION POEMS PER SIN MUTED GUY
PER SIN POEMS BRION MUTED GUY
SIN POEMS PER BRION MUTED GUY

PER BRION SIN POEMS MUTED GUY
SIN PER BRION POEMS MUTED GUY
POEMS BRION SIN PER MUTED GUY
SIN POEMS BRION PER MUTED GUY
MUTED POEMS BRION SIN PER GUY
BRION MUTED POEMS SIN PER GUY
MUTED POEMS SIN BRION PER GUY
SIN MUTED POEMS BRION PER GUY
MUTED BRION SIN POEMS PER GUY
SIN MUTED BRION POEMS PER GUY
POEMS BRION SIN MUTED PER GUY
SIN POEMS BRION MUTED PER GUY
PER MUTED POEMS GUY SIN BRION
POEMS PER MUTED GUY SIN BRION
PER MUTED GUY POEMS SIN BRION
GUY PER MUTED POEMS SIN BRION
PER POEMS GUY MUTED SIN BRION
GUY PER POEMS MUTED SIN BRION
MUTED POEMS GUY PER SIN BRION
GUY MUTED POEMS PER SIN BRION
PER MUTED POEMS SIN GUY BRION
POEMS PER MUTED SIN GUY BRION
PER MUTED SIN POEMS GUY BRION
SIN PER MUTED POEMS GUY BRION
PER POEMS SIN MUTED GUY BRION
SIN PER POEMS MUTED GUY BRION
MUTED POEMS SIN PER GUY BRION
SIN MUTED POEMS PER GUY BRION
PER MUTED GUY SIN POEMS BRION
GUY PER MUTED SIN POEMS BRION
PER MUTED SIN GUY POEMS BRION
SIN PER MUTED GUY POEMS BRION
PER GUY SIN MUTED POEMS BRION
SIN PER GUY MUTED POEMS BRION
MUTED GUY SIN PER POEMS BRION
SIN MUTED GUY PER POEMS BRION
PER POEMS GUY SIN MUTED BRION
GUY PER POEMS SIN MUTED BRION
PER POEMS SIN GUY MUTED BRION
SIN PER POEMS GUY MUTED BRION
PER GUY SIN POEMS MUTED BRION
SIN PER GUY POEMS MUTED BRION
POEMS GUY SIN PER MUTED BRION
SIN POEMS GUY PER MUTED BRION
MUTED POEMS GUY SIN PER BRION
GUY MUTED POEMS SIN PER BRION
MUTED POEMS SIN GUY PER BRION
SIN MUTED POEMS GUY PER BRION
MUTED GUY SIN POEMS PER BRION
SIN MUTED GUY POEMS PER BRION
POEMS GUY SIN MUTED PER BRION
SIN POEMS GUY MUTED PER BRION
PER MUTED BRION GUY SIN POEMS
BRION PER MUTED GUY SIN POEMS
PER MUTED GUY BRION SIN POEMS
GUY PER MUTED BRION SIN POEMS
PER BRION GUY MUTED SIN POEMS
GUY PER BRION MUTED SIN POEMS
MUTED BRION GUY PER SIN POEMS
GUY MUTED BRION PER SIN POEMS
PER MUTED BRION SIN GUY POEMS
BRION PER MUTED SIN GUY POEMS
PER MUTED SIN BRION GUY POEMS
SIN PER MUTED BRION GUY POEMS
PER BRION SIN MUTED GUY POEMS
SIN PER BRION MUTED GUY POEMS
MUTED BRION SIN PER GUY POEMS
SIN MUTED BRION PER GUY POEMS

BRION PER SIN POEMS MUTED GUY
BRION SIN PER POEMS MUTED GUY
BRION POEMS SIN PER MUTED GUY
BRION SIN POEMS PER MUTED GUY
POEMS MUTED BRION SIN PER GUY
POEMS BRION MUTED SIN PER GUY
POEMS MUTED SIN BRION PER GUY
POEMS SIN MUTED BRION PER GUY
BRION MUTED SIN POEMS PER GUY
BRION SIN MUTED POEMS PER GUY
BRION POEMS SIN MUTED PER GUY
BRION SIN POEMS MUTED PER GUY
MUTED PER POEMS GUY SIN BRION
MUTED POEMS PER GUY SIN BRION
MUTED PER GUY POEMS SIN BRION
MUTED GUY PER POEMS SIN BRION
POEMS PER GUY MUTED SIN BRION
POEMS GUY PER MUTED SIN BRION
POEMS MUTED GUY PER SIN BRION
POEMS GUY MUTED PER SIN BRION
MUTED PER POEMS SIN GUY BRION
MUTED POEMS PER SIN GUY BRION
MUTED PER SIN POEMS GUY BRION
MUTED SIN PER POEMS GUY BRION
POEMS PER SIN MUTED GUY BRION
POEMS SIN PER MUTED GUY BRION
POEMS MUTED SIN PER GUY BRION
POEMS SIN MUTED PER GUY BRION
MUTED PER GUY SIN POEMS BRION
MUTED GUY PER SIN POEMS BRION
MUTED PER SIN GUY POEMS BRION
MUTED SIN PER GUY POEMS BRION
GUY PER SIN MUTED POEMS BRION
GUY SIN PER MUTED POEMS BRION
GUY MUTED SIN PER POEMS BRION
GUY SIN MUTED PER POEMS BRION
POEMS PER GUY SIN MUTED BRION
POEMS GUY PER SIN MUTED BRION
POEMS PER SIN GUY MUTED BRION
POEMS SIN PER GUY MUTED BRION
GUY PER SIN POEMS MUTED BRION
GUY SIN PER POEMS MUTED BRION
GUY POEMS SIN PER MUTED BRION
GUY SIN POEMS PER MUTED BRION
POEMS MUTED GUY SIN PER BRION
POEMS GUY MUTED SIN PER BRION
POEMS MUTED SIN GUY PER BRION
POEMS SIN MUTED GUY PER BRION
GUY MUTED SIN POEMS PER BRION
GUY SIN MUTED POEMS PER BRION
GUY POEMS SIN MUTED PER BRION
GUY SIN POEMS MUTED PER BRION
MUTED PER BRION GUY SIN POEMS
MUTED BRION PER GUY SIN POEMS
MUTED PER GUY BRION SIN POEMS
MUTED GUY PER BRION SIN POEMS
BRION PER GUY MUTED SIN POEMS
BRION GUY PER MUTED SIN POEMS
BRION MUTED GUY PER SIN POEMS
BRION GUY MUTED PER SIN POEMS
MUTED PER BRION SIN GUY POEMS
MUTED BRION PER SIN GUY POEMS
MUTED PER SIN BRION GUY POEMS
MUTED SIN PER BRION GUY POEMS
BRION PER SIN MUTED GUY POEMS
BRION SIN PER MUTED GUY POEMS
BRION MUTED SIN PER GUY POEMS
BRION SIN MUTED PER GUY POEMS

PER SIN BRION POEMS MUTED GUY
SIN BRION PER POEMS MUTED GUY
POEMS SIN BRION PER MUTED GUY
SIN BRION POEMS PER MUTED GUY
MUTED BRION POEMS SIN PER GUY
BRION POEMS MUTED SIN PER GUY
MUTED SIN POEMS BRION PER GUY
SIN POEMS MUTED BRION PER GUY
MUTED SIN BRION POEMS PER GUY
SIN BRION MUTED POEMS PER GUY
POEMS SIN BRION MUTED PER GUY
SIN BRION POEMS MUTED PER GUY
PER POEMS MUTED GUY SIN BRION
POEMS MUTED PER GUY SIN BRION
PER GUY MUTED POEMS SIN BRION
GUY MUTED PER POEMS SIN BRION
PER GUY POEMS MUTED SIN BRION
GUY POEMS PER MUTED SIN BRION
MUTED GUY POEMS PER SIN BRION
GUY POEMS MUTED PER SIN BRION
PER POEMS MUTED SIN GUY BRION
POEMS MUTED PER SIN GUY BRION
PER SIN MUTED POEMS GUY BRION
SIN MUTED PER POEMS GUY BRION
PER SIN POEMS MUTED GUY BRION
SIN POEMS PER MUTED GUY BRION
MUTED SIN POEMS PER GUY BRION
SIN POEMS MUTED PER GUY BRION
PER GUY MUTED SIN POEMS BRION
GUY MUTED PER SIN POEMS BRION
PER SIN MUTED GUY POEMS BRION
SIN MUTED PER GUY POEMS BRION
PER SIN GUY MUTED POEMS BRION
SIN GUY PER MUTED POEMS BRION
MUTED SIN GUY PER POEMS BRION
SIN GUY MUTED PER POEMS BRION
PER GUY POEMS SIN MUTED BRION
GUY POEMS PER SIN MUTED BRION
PER SIN POEMS GUY MUTED BRION
SIN POEMS PER GUY MUTED BRION
PER SIN GUY POEMS MUTED BRION
SIN GUY PER POEMS MUTED BRION
POEMS SIN GUY PER MUTED BRION
SIN GUY POEMS PER MUTED BRION
MUTED GUY POEMS SIN PER BRION
GUY POEMS MUTED SIN PER BRION
MUTED SIN POEMS GUY PER BRION
SIN POEMS MUTED GUY PER BRION
MUTED SIN GUY POEMS PER BRION
SIN GUY MUTED POEMS PER BRION
POEMS SIN GUY MUTED PER BRION
SIN GUY POEMS MUTED PER BRION
PER BRION MUTED GUY SIN POEMS
BRION MUTED PER GUY SIN POEMS
PER GUY MUTED BRION SIN POEMS
GUY MUTED PER BRION SIN POEMS
PER GUY BRION MUTED SIN POEMS
GUY BRION PER MUTED SIN POEMS
MUTED GUY BRION PER SIN POEMS
GUY BRION MUTED PER SIN POEMS
PER BRION MUTED SIN GUY POEMS
BRION MUTED PER SIN GUY POEMS
PER SIN MUTED BRION GUY POEMS
SIN MUTED PER BRION GUY POEMS
PER SIN BRION MUTED GUY POEMS
SIN BRION PER MUTED GUY POEMS
MUTED SIN BRION PER GUY POEMS
SIN BRION MUTED PER GUY POEMS

PER MUTED GUY SIN BRION POEMS
GUY PER MUTED SIN BRION POEMS
PER MUTED SIN GUY BRION POEMS
SIN PER MUTED GUY BRION POEMS
PER GUY SIN MUTED BRION POEMS
SIN PER GUY MUTED BRION POEMS
MUTED GUY SIN PER BRION POEMS
SIN MUTED GUY PER BRION POEMS
PER BRION GUY SIN MUTED POEMS
GUY PER BRION SIN MUTED POEMS
PER BRION SIN GUY MUTED POEMS
SIN PER BRION GUY MUTED POEMS
PER GUY SIN BRION MUTED POEMS
SIN PER GUY BRION MUTED POEMS
BRION GUY SIN PER MUTED POEMS
SIN BRION GUY PER MUTED POEMS
MUTED BRION GUY SIN PER POEMS
GUY MUTED BRION SIN PER POEMS
MUTED BRION SIN GUY PER POEMS
SIN MUTED BRION GUY PER POEMS
MUTED GUY SIN BRION PER POEMS
SIN MUTED GUY BRION PER POEMS
BRION GUY SIN MUTED PER POEMS
SIN BRION GUY MUTED PER POEMS
PER POEMS BRION GUY SIN MUTED
BRION PER POEMS GUY SIN MUTED
PER POEMS GUY BRION SIN MUTED
GUY PER POEMS BRION SIN MUTED
PER BRION GUY POEMS SIN MUTED
GUY PER BRION POEMS SIN MUTED
POEMS BRION GUY PER SIN MUTED
GUY POEMS BRION PER SIN MUTED
PER POEMS BRION SIN GUY MUTED
BRION PER POEMS SIN GUY MUTED
PER POEMS SIN BRION GUY MUTED
SIN PER POEMS BRION GUY MUTED
PER BRION SIN POEMS GUY MUTED
SIN PER BRION POEMS GUY MUTED
POEMS BRION SIN PER GUY MUTED
SIN POEMS BRION PER GUY MUTED
PER POEMS GUY SIN BRION MUTED
GUY PER POEMS SIN BRION MUTED
PER POEMS SIN GUY BRION MUTED
SIN PER POEMS GUY BRION MUTED
PER GUY SIN POEMS BRION MUTED
SIN PER GUY POEMS BRION MUTED
POEMS GUY SIN PER BRION MUTED
SIN POEMS GUY PER BRION MUTED
PER BRION GUY SIN POEMS MUTED
GUY PER BRION SIN POEMS MUTED
PER BRION SIN GUY POEMS MUTED
SIN PER BRION GUY POEMS MUTED
PER GUY SIN BRION POEMS MUTED
SIN PER GUY BRION POEMS MUTED
BRION GUY SIN PER POEMS MUTED
SIN BRION GUY PER POEMS MUTED
POEMS BRION GUY SIN PER MUTED
GUY POEMS BRION SIN PER MUTED
POEMS BRION SIN GUY PER MUTED
SIN POEMS BRION GUY PER MUTED
POEMS GUY SIN BRION PER MUTED
SIN POEMS GUY BRION PER MUTED
BRION GUY SIN POEMS PER MUTED
SIN BRION GUY POEMS PER MUTED
MUTED POEMS BRION GUY SIN PER
BRION MUTED POEMS GUY SIN PER
MUTED POEMS GUY BRION SIN PER
GUY MUTED POEMS BRION SIN PER

MUTED PER GUY SIN BRION POEMS
MUTED GUY PER SIN BRION POEMS
MUTED PER SIN GUY BRION POEMS
MUTED SIN PER GUY BRION POEMS
GUY PER SIN MUTED BRION POEMS
GUY SIN PER MUTED BRION POEMS
GUY MUTED SIN PER BRION POEMS
GUY SIN MUTED PER BRION POEMS
BRION PER GUY SIN MUTED POEMS
BRION GUY PER SIN MUTED POEMS
BRION PER SIN GUY MUTED POEMS
BRION SIN PER GUY MUTED POEMS
GUY PER SIN BRION MUTED POEMS
GUY SIN PER BRION MUTED POEMS
GUY BRION SIN PER MUTED POEMS
GUY SIN BRION PER MUTED POEMS
BRION MUTED GUY SIN PER POEMS
BRION GUY MUTED SIN PER POEMS
BRION MUTED SIN GUY PER POEMS
BRION SIN MUTED GUY PER POEMS
GUY MUTED SIN BRION PER POEMS
GUY SIN MUTED BRION PER POEMS
GUY BRION SIN MUTED PER POEMS
GUY SIN BRION MUTED PER POEMS
POEMS PER BRION GUY SIN MUTED
POEMS BRION PER GUY SIN MUTED
POEMS PER GUY BRION SIN MUTED
POEMS GUY PER BRION SIN MUTED
BRION PER GUY POEMS SIN MUTED
BRION GUY PER POEMS SIN MUTED
BRION POEMS GUY PER SIN MUTED
BRION GUY POEMS PER SIN MUTED
POEMS PER BRION SIN GUY MUTED
POEMS BRION PER SIN GUY MUTED
POEMS PER SIN BRION GUY MUTED
POEMS SIN PER BRION GUY MUTED
BRION PER SIN POEMS GUY MUTED
BRION SIN PER POEMS GUY MUTED
BRION POEMS SIN PER GUY MUTED
BRION SIN POEMS PER GUY MUTED
POEMS PER GUY SIN BRION MUTED
POEMS GUY PER SIN BRION MUTED
POEMS PER SIN GUY BRION MUTED
POEMS SIN PER GUY BRION MUTED
GUY PER SIN POEMS BRION MUTED
GUY SIN PER POEMS BRION MUTED
GUY POEMS SIN PER BRION MUTED
GUY SIN POEMS PER BRION MUTED
BRION PER GUY SIN POEMS MUTED
BRION GUY PER SIN POEMS MUTED
BRION PER SIN GUY POEMS MUTED
BRION SIN PER GUY POEMS MUTED
GUY PER SIN BRION POEMS MUTED
GUY SIN PER BRION POEMS MUTED
GUY BRION SIN PER POEMS MUTED
GUY SIN BRION PER POEMS MUTED
BRION POEMS GUY SIN PER MUTED
BRION GUY POEMS SIN PER MUTED
BRION POEMS SIN GUY PER MUTED
BRION SIN POEMS GUY PER MUTED
GUY POEMS SIN BRION PER MUTED
GUY SIN POEMS BRION PER MUTED
GUY BRION SIN POEMS PER MUTED
GUY SIN BRION POEMS PER MUTED
POEMS MUTED BRION GUY SIN PER
POEMS BRION MUTED GUY SIN PER
POEMS MUTED GUY BRION SIN PER
POEMS GUY MUTED BRION SIN PER

PER GUY MUTED SIN BRION POEMS
GUY MUTED PER SIN BRION POEMS
PER SIN MUTED GUY BRION POEMS
SIN MUTED PER GUY BRION POEMS
PER SIN GUY MUTED BRION POEMS
SIN GUY PER MUTED BRION POEMS
MUTED SIN GUY PER BRION POEMS
SIN GUY MUTED PER BRION POEMS
PER GUY BRION SIN MUTED POEMS
GUY BRION PER SIN MUTED POEMS
PER SIN BRION GUY MUTED POEMS
SIN BRION PER GUY MUTED POEMS
PER SIN GUY BRION MUTED POEMS
SIN GUY PER BRION MUTED POEMS
BRION SIN GUY PER MUTED POEMS
SIN GUY BRION PER MUTED POEMS
MUTED GUY BRION SIN PER POEMS
GUY BRION MUTED SIN PER POEMS
MUTED SIN BRION GUY PER POEMS
SIN BRION MUTED GUY PER POEMS
MUTED SIN GUY BRION PER POEMS
SIN GUY MUTED BRION PER POEMS
BRION SIN GUY MUTED PER POEMS
SIN GUY BRION MUTED PER POEMS
PER BRION POEMS GUY SIN MUTED
BRION POEMS PER GUY SIN MUTED
PER GUY POEMS BRION SIN MUTED
GUY POEMS PER BRION SIN MUTED
PER GUY BRION POEMS SIN MUTED
GUY BRION PER POEMS SIN MUTED
POEMS GUY BRION PER SIN MUTED
GUY BRION POEMS PER SIN MUTED
PER BRION POEMS SIN GUY MUTED
BRION POEMS PER SIN GUY MUTED
PER SIN POEMS BRION GUY MUTED
SIN POEMS PER BRION GUY MUTED
PER SIN BRION POEMS GUY MUTED
SIN BRION PER POEMS GUY MUTED
POEMS SIN BRION PER GUY MUTED
SIN BRION POEMS PER GUY MUTED
PER GUY POEMS SIN BRION MUTED
GUY POEMS PER SIN BRION MUTED
PER SIN POEMS GUY BRION MUTED
SIN POEMS PER GUY BRION MUTED
PER SIN GUY POEMS BRION MUTED
SIN GUY PER POEMS BRION MUTED
POEMS SIN GUY PER BRION MUTED
SIN GUY POEMS PER BRION MUTED
PER GUY BRION SIN POEMS MUTED
GUY BRION PER SIN POEMS MUTED
PER SIN BRION GUY POEMS MUTED
SIN BRION PER GUY POEMS MUTED
PER SIN GUY BRION POEMS MUTED
SIN GUY PER BRION POEMS MUTED
BRION SIN GUY PER POEMS MUTED
SIN GUY BRION PER POEMS MUTED
POEMS GUY BRION SIN PER MUTED
GUY BRION POEMS SIN PER MUTED
POEMS SIN BRION GUY PER MUTED
SIN BRION POEMS GUY PER MUTED
POEMS SIN GUY BRION PER MUTED
SIN GUY POEMS BRION PER MUTED
BRION SIN GUY POEMS PER MUTED
SIN GUY BRION POEMS PER MUTED
MUTED BRION POEMS GUY SIN PER
BRION POEMS MUTED GUY SIN PER
MUTED GUY POEMS BRION SIN PER
GUY POEMS MUTED BRION SIN PER

MUTED BRION GUY POEMS SIN PER
GUY MUTED BRION POEMS SIN PER
POEMS BRION GUY MUTED SIN PER
GUY POEMS BRION MUTED SIN PER
MUTED POEMS BRION SIN GUY PER
BRION MUTED POEMS SIN GUY PER
MUTED POEMS SIN BRION GUY PER
SIN MUTED POEMS BRION GUY PER
MUTED BRION SIN POEMS GUY PER
SIN MUTED BRION POEMS GUY PER
POEMS BRION SIN MUTED GUY PER
SIN POEMS BRION MUTED GUY PER
MUTED POEMS GUY SIN BRION PER
GUY MUTED POEMS SIN BRION PER
MUTED POEMS SIN GUY BRION PER
SIN MUTED POEMS GUY BRION PER
MUTED GUY SIN POEMS BRION PER
SIN MUTED GUY POEMS BRION PER
POEMS GUY SIN MUTED BRION PER
SIN POEMS GUY MUTED BRION PER
MUTED BRION GUY SIN POEMS PER
GUY MUTED BRION SIN POEMS PER
MUTED BRION SIN GUY POEMS PER
SIN MUTED BRION GUY POEMS PER
MUTED GUY SIN BRION POEMS PER
SIN MUTED GUY BRION POEMS PER
BRION GUY SIN MUTED POEMS PER
SIN BRION GUY MUTED POEMS PER
POEMS BRION GUY SIN MUTED PER
GUY POEMS BRION SIN MUTED PER
POEMS BRION SIN GUY MUTED PER
SIN POEMS BRION GUY MUTED PER
POEMS GUY SIN BRION MUTED PER
SIN POEMS GUY BRION MUTED PER
BRION GUY SIN POEMS MUTED PER
SIN BRION GUY POEMS MUTED PER

BRION MUTED GUY POEMS SIN PER
BRION GUY MUTED POEMS SIN PER
BRION POEMS GUY MUTED SIN PER
BRION GUY POEMS MUTED SIN PER
POEMS MUTED BRION SIN GUY PER
POEMS BRION MUTED SIN GUY PER
POEMS MUTED SIN BRION GUY PER
POEMS SIN MUTED BRION GUY PER
BRION MUTED SIN POEMS GUY PER
BRION SIN MUTED POEMS GUY PER
BRION POEMS SIN MUTED GUY PER
BRION SIN POEMS MUTED GUY PER
POEMS MUTED GUY SIN BRION PER
POEMS GUY MUTED SIN BRION PER
POEMS MUTED SIN GUY BRION PER
POEMS SIN MUTED GUY BRION PER
GUY MUTED SIN POEMS BRION PER
GUY SIN MUTED POEMS BRION PER
GUY POEMS SIN MUTED BRION PER
GUY SIN POEMS MUTED BRION PER
BRION MUTED GUY SIN POEMS PER
BRION GUY MUTED SIN POEMS PER
BRION MUTED SIN GUY POEMS PER
BRION SIN MUTED GUY POEMS PER
GUY MUTED SIN BRION POEMS PER
GUY SIN MUTED BRION POEMS PER
GUY BRION SIN MUTED POEMS PER
GUY SIN BRION MUTED POEMS PER
BRION POEMS GUY SIN MUTED PER
BRION GUY POEMS SIN MUTED PER
BRION POEMS SIN GUY MUTED PER
BRION SIN POEMS GUY MUTED PER
GUY POEMS SIN BRION MUTED PER
GUY SIN POEMS BRION MUTED PER
GUY BRION SIN POEMS MUTED PER
GUY SIN BRION POEMS MUTED PER

MUTED GUY BRION POEMS SIN PER
GUY BRION MUTED POEMS SIN PER
POEMS GUY BRION MUTED SIN PER
GUY BRION POEMS MUTED SIN PER
MUTED BRION POEMS SIN GUY PER
BRION POEMS MUTED SIN GUY PER
MUTED SIN POEMS BRION GUY PER
SIN POEMS MUTED BRION GUY PER
MUTED SIN BRION POEMS GUY PER
SIN BRION MUTED POEMS GUY PER
POEMS SIN BRION MUTED GUY PER
SIN BRION POEMS MUTED GUY PER
MUTED GUY POEMS SIN BRION PER
GUY POEMS MUTED SIN BRION PER
MUTED SIN POEMS GUY BRION PER
SIN POEMS MUTED GUY BRION PER
MUTED SIN GUY POEMS BRION PER
SIN GUY MUTED POEMS BRION PER
POEMS SIN GUY MUTED BRION PER
SIN GUY POEMS MUTED BRION PER
MUTED GUY BRION SIN POEMS PER
GUY BRION MUTED SIN POEMS PER
MUTED SIN BRION GUY POEMS PER
SIN BRION MUTED GUY POEMS PER
MUTED SIN GUY BRION POEMS PER
SIN GUY MUTED BRION POEMS PER
BRION SIN GUY MUTED POEMS PER
SIN GUY BRION MUTED POEMS PER
POEMS GUY BRION SIN MUTED PER
GUY BRION POEMS SIN MUTED PER
POEMS SIN BRION GUY MUTED PER
SIN BRION POEMS GUY MUTED PER
POEMS SIN GUY BRION MUTED PER
SIN GUY POEMS BRION MUTED PER
BRION SIN GUY POEMS MUTED PER
SIN GUY BRION POEMS MUTED PER

BRION THEREFORE I I THINK AM GYSIN $ *) – . (£
THEREFORE BRION I I THINK AM GYSIN   * $) – . (£
BRION I THEREFORE I THINK AM GYSIN $) * – . (£
I BRION THEREFORE I THINK AM GYSIN   ) $ * – . (£
THEREFORE I BRION I THINK AM GYSIN   *) $ – . (£
I THEREFORE BRION I THINK AM GYSIN   ) * $ – . (£
I THEREFORE I BRION THINK AM GYSIN   – *) $. (£
THEREFORE I I BRION THINK AM GYSIN   * –) $. (£
I I THEREFORE BRION THINK AM GYSIN   –) * $. (£
I I THEREFORE BRION THINK AM GYSIN   ) – * $. (£
THEREFORE I I BRION THINK AM GYSIN   *) – $. (£
I THEREFORE I BRION THINK AM GYSIN   ) * – $. (£
BRION THINK THEREFORE I I AM GYSIN $. *) – (£
THINK BRION THEREFORE I I AM GYSIN   . $ *) – (£
BRION THEREFORE THINK I I AM GYSIN $ * .) – (£
THEREFORE BRION THINK I I AM GYSIN   * $.) – (£
THINK THEREFORE BRION I I AM GYSIN   . * $) – (£
THEREFORE THINK BRION I I AM GYSIN   * . $) – (£
BRION THINK I THEREFORE I AM GYSIN $.) * – (£
THINK BRION I THEREFORE I AM GYSIN   . $) * – (£
BRION I THINK THEREFORE I AM GYSIN $) . * – (£
I BRION THINK THEREFORE I AM GYSIN   ) $. * – (£
THINK I BRION THEREFORE I AM GYSIN   .) $ * – (£
I THINK BRION THEREFORE I AM GYSIN   ) . $ * – (£
BRION THEREFORE I THINK I AM GYSIN $ *) . – (£
THEREFORE BRION I THINK I AM GYSIN   * $) . – (£
BRION I THEREFORE THINK I AM GYSIN $) * . – (£
I BRION THEREFORE THINK I AM GYSIN   ) $ * . – (£
THEREFORE I BRION THINK I AM GYSIN   *) $. – (£
I THEREFORE BRION THINK I AM GYSIN   ) * $. – (£
THINK THEREFORE I BRION I AM GYSIN   . *) $ – (£
THEREFORE THINK I BRION I AM GYSIN   * .) $ – (£
THINK I THEREFORE BRION I AM GYSIN   .) * $ – (£
I THINK THEREFORE BRION I AM GYSIN   ) . * $ – (£
THEREFORE I THINK BRION I AM GYSIN   *) . $ – (£
I THEREFORE THINK BRION I AM GYSIN   ) * . $ – (£
I THINK THEREFORE I BRION AM GYSIN   – . *) $ (£
THINK I THEREFORE I BRION AM GYSIN   . – *) $ (£
I THEREFORE THINK I BRION AM GYSIN   – * .) $ (£
THEREFORE I THINK I BRION AM GYSIN   * – .) $ (£
THINK THEREFORE I I BRION AM GYSIN   . * –) $ (£
THEREFORE THINK I I BRION AM GYSIN   * . –) $ (£
I THINK I THEREFORE BRION AM GYSIN   – .) * $ (£
THINK I I THEREFORE BRION AM GYSIN   . –) * $ (£
I I THINK THEREFORE BRION AM GYSIN   –) . * $ (£
I I THINK THEREFORE BRION AM GYSIN   ) – . * $ (£
THINK I I THEREFORE BRION AM GYSIN   .) – * $ (£
I THINK I THEREFORE BRION AM GYSIN   ) . – * $ (£
I THEREFORE I THINK BRION AM GYSIN   – *) . $ (£
THEREFORE I I THINK BRION AM GYSIN   * –) . $ (£
I I THEREFORE THINK BRION AM GYSIN   –) * . $ (£
I I THEREFORE THINK BRION AM GYSIN   ) – * . $ (£
THEREFORE I I THINK BRION AM GYSIN   *) – . $ (£
I THEREFORE I THINK BRION AM GYSIN   ) * – . $ (£
THINK THEREFORE I I BRION AM GYSIN   . *) – $ (£
THEREFORE THINK I I BRION AM GYSIN   * .) – $ (£
THINK I THEREFORE I BRION AM GYSIN   .) * – $ (£
I THINK THEREFORE I BRION AM GYSIN   ) . * – $ (£
THEREFORE I THINK I BRION AM GYSIN   *) . – $ (£
I THEREFORE THINK I BRION AM GYSIN   ) * . – $ (£

AM I THINK THEREFORE I BRION GYSIN (– . *) $ £
I AM THINK THEREFORE I BRION GYSIN – (. *) $ £
AM THINK I THEREFORE I BRION GYSIN (. – *) $ £
THINK AM I THEREFORE I BRION GYSIN . (– *) $ £
I THINK AM THEREFORE I BRION GYSIN – . (*) $ £
THINK I AM THEREFORE I BRION GYSIN . – (*) $ £
AM I THEREFORE THINK I BRION GYSIN (– * .) $ £
I AM THEREFORE THINK I BRION GYSIN – (* .) $ £
AM THEREFORE I THINK I BRION GYSIN (* – .) $ £
THEREFORE AM I THINK I BRION GYSIN * (– .) $ £
I THEREFORE AM THINK I BRION GYSIN – * (.) $ £
THEREFORE I AM THINK I BRION GYSIN * – (.) $ £
AM THINK THEREFORE I I BRION GYSIN (. * –) $ £
THINK AM THEREFORE I I BRION GYSIN . (* –) $ £
AM THEREFORE THINK I I BRION GYSIN (* . –) $ £
THEREFORE AM THINK I I BRION GYSIN * (. –) $ £
THINK THEREFORE AM I I BRION GYSIN . * (–) $ £
THEREFORE THINK AM I I BRION GYSIN * . (–) $ £
I THINK THEREFORE AM I BRION GYSIN – . * ( ) $ £
THINK I THEREFORE AM I BRION GYSIN . – * ( ) $ £
I THEREFORE THINK AM I BRION GYSIN – * . ( ) $ £
THEREFORE I THINK AM I BRION GYSIN * – . ( ) $ £
THINK THEREFORE I AM I BRION GYSIN . * – ( ) $ £
THEREFORE THINK I AM I BRION GYSIN * . – ( ) $ £
AM I THINK I THEREFORE BRION GYSIN (– .) * $ £
I AM THINK I THEREFORE BRION GYSIN – (.) * $ £
AM THINK I I THEREFORE BRION GYSIN (. –) * $ £
THINK AM I I THEREFORE BRION GYSIN . (–) * $ £
I THINK AM I THEREFORE BRION GYSIN – . ( ) * $ £
THINK I AM I THEREFORE BRION GYSIN . – ( ) * $ £
AM I I THINK THEREFORE BRION GYSIN (–) . * $ £
I AM I THINK THEREFORE BRION GYSIN – ( ) . * $ £
AM I I THINK THEREFORE BRION GYSIN ( ) – . * $ £
I AM I THINK THEREFORE BRION GYSIN) (– . * $ £
I I AM THINK THEREFORE BRION GYSIN –) (. * $ £
I I AM THINK THEREFORE BRION GYSIN) – (. * $ £
AM THINK I I THEREFORE BRION GYSIN (.) – * $ £
THINK AM I I THEREFORE BRION GYSIN . ( ) – * $ £
AM I THINK I THEREFORE BRION GYSIN ( ) . – * $ £
I AM THINK I THEREFORE BRION GYSIN) (. – * $ £
THINK I AM I THEREFORE BRION GYSIN .) (– * $ £
I THINK AM I THEREFORE BRION GYSIN) . (– * $ £
I THINK I AM THEREFORE BRION GYSIN – .) (* $ £
THINK I I AM THEREFORE BRION GYSIN . –) (* $ £
I I THINK AM THEREFORE BRION GYSIN –) . (* $ £
I I THINK AM THEREFORE BRION GYSIN) – . (* $ £
THINK I I AM THEREFORE BRION GYSIN .) – (* $ £
I THINK I AM THEREFORE BRION GYSIN) . – (* $ £
AM I THEREFORE I THINK BRION GYSIN (– *) . $ £
I AM THEREFORE I THINK BRION GYSIN – (*) . $ £
AM THEREFORE I I THINK BRION GYSIN (* –) . $ £
THEREFORE AM I I THINK BRION GYSIN * (–) . $ £
I THEREFORE AM I THINK BRION GYSIN – * ( ) . $ £
THEREFORE I AM I THINK BRION GYSIN * – ( ) . $ £
AM I I THEREFORE THINK BRION GYSIN (–) * . $ £
I AM I THEREFORE THINK BRION GYSIN – ( ) * . $ £
AM I I THEREFORE THINK BRION GYSIN ( ) – * . $ £
I AM I THEREFORE THINK BRION GYSIN) (– * . $ £
I I AM THEREFORE THINK BRION GYSIN –) (* . $ £
I I AM THEREFORE THINK BRION GYSIN) – (* . $ £

AM THEREFORE I I THINK BRION GYSIN (*) - . $ £
THEREFORE AM I I THINK BRION GYSIN * ( ) - . $ £
AM I THEREFORE I THINK BRION GYSIN ( ) * - . $ £
I AM THEREFORE I THINK BRION GYSIN) (* - . $ £
THEREFORE I AM I THINK BRION GYSIN *) (- . $ £
I THEREFORE AM I THINK BRION GYSIN) * (- . $ £
I THEREFORE I AM THINK BRION GYSIN - *) (. $ £
THEREFORE I I AM THINK BRION GYSIN * -) (. $ £
I I THEREFORE AM THINK BRION GYSIN -) * (. $ £
I I THEREFORE AM THINK BRION GYSIN) - * (. $ £
THEREFORE I I AM THINK BRION GYSIN *) - (. $ £
I THEREFORE I AM THINK BRION GYSIN) * - (. $ £
AM THINK THEREFORE I I BRION GYSIN (. *) - $ £
THINK AM THEREFORE I I BRION GYSIN . (*) - $ £
AM THEREFORE THINK I I BRION GYSIN (* .) - $ £
THEREFORE AM THINK I I BRION GYSIN * (.) - $ £
THINK THEREFORE AM I I BRION GYSIN . * ( ) - $ £
THEREFORE THINK AM I I BRION GYSIN * . ( ) - $ £
AM THINK I THEREFORE I BRION GYSIN (.) * - $ £
THINK AM I THEREFORE I BRION GYSIN . ( ) * - $ £
AM I THINK THEREFORE I BRION GYSIN ( ) . * - $ £
I AM THINK THEREFORE I BRION GYSIN) (. * - $ £
THINK I AM THEREFORE I BRION GYSIN .) (* - $ £
I THINK AM THEREFORE I BRION GYSIN) . (* - $ £
AM THEREFORE I THINK I BRION GYSIN (*) . - $ £
THEREFORE AM I THINK I BRION GYSIN * ( ) . - $ £
AM I THEREFORE THINK I BRION GYSIN ( ) * . - $ £
I AM THEREFORE THINK I BRION GYSIN) (* . - $ £
THEREFORE I AM THINK I BRION GYSIN *) (. - $ £
I THEREFORE AM THINK I BRION GYSIN) * (. - $ £
THINK THEREFORE I AM I BRION GYSIN . *) (- $ £
THEREFORE THINK I AM I BRION GYSIN * .) (- $ £
THINK I THEREFORE AM I BRION GYSIN .) * (- $ £
I THINK THEREFORE AM I BRION GYSIN) . * (- $ £
THEREFORE I THINK AM I BRION GYSIN *) . (- $ £
I THEREFORE THINK AM I BRION GYSIN) * . (- $ £
I THINK THEREFORE I AM BRION GYSIN - . *) ($ £
THINK I THEREFORE I AM BRION GYSIN . - *) ($ £
I THEREFORE THINK I AM BRION GYSIN - * .) ($ £
THEREFORE I THINK I AM BRION GYSIN * - .) ($ £
THINK THEREFORE I I AM BRION GYSIN . * -) ($ £
THEREFORE THINK I I AM BRION GYSIN * . -) ($ £
I THINK I THEREFORE AM BRION GYSIN - .) * ($ £
THINK I I THEREFORE AM BRION GYSIN . -) * ($ £
I I THINK THEREFORE AM BRION GYSIN -) . * ($ £
I I THINK THEREFORE AM BRION GYSIN) - . * ($ £
THINK I I THEREFORE AM BRION GYSIN .) - * ($ £
I THINK I THEREFORE AM BRION GYSIN) . - * ($ £
I THEREFORE I THINK AM BRION GYSIN - *) . ($ £
THEREFORE I I THINK AM BRION GYSIN * -) . ($ £
I I THEREFORE THINK AM BRION GYSIN -) * . ($ £
I I THEREFORE THINK AM BRION GYSIN) - * . ($ £
THEREFORE I I THINK AM BRION GYSIN *) - . ($ £
I THEREFORE I THINK AM BRION GYSIN) * - . ($ £
THINK THEREFORE I I AM BRION GYSIN . *) - ($ £
THEREFORE THINK I I AM BRION GYSIN * .) - ($ £
THINK I THEREFORE I AM BRION GYSIN .) * - ($ £
I THINK THEREFORE I AM BRION GYSIN) . * - ($ £
THEREFORE I THINK I AM BRION GYSIN *) . - ($ £
I THEREFORE THINK I AM BRION GYSIN) * . - ($ £

THIS IS WILLIAM S. BURROUGHS
IS THIS WILLIAM S. BURROUGHS
THIS WILLIAM IS S. BURROUGHS
WILLIAM THIS IS S. BURROUGHS
IS WILLIAM THIS S. BURROUGHS
WILLIAM IS THIS S. BURROUGHS
THIS IS S. WILLIAM BURROUGHS
IS THIS S. WILLIAM BURROUGHS
THIS S. IS WILLIAM BURROUGHS
S. THIS IS WILLIAM BURROUGHS
IS S. THIS WILLIAM BURROUGHS
S. IS THIS WILLIAM BURROUGHS
THIS WILLIAM S. IS BURROUGHS
WILLIAM THIS S. IS BURROUGHS
THIS S. WILLIAM IS BURROUGHS
S. THIS WILLIAM IS BURROUGHS
WILLIAM S. THIS IS BURROUGHS
S. WILLIAM THIS IS BURROUGHS
IS WILLIAM S. THIS BURROUGHS
WILLIAM IS S. THIS BURROUGHS
IS S. WILLIAM THIS BURROUGHS
S. IS WILLIAM THIS BURROUGHS
WILLIAM S. IS THIS BURROUGHS
S. WILLIAM IS THIS BURROUGHS
THIS IS WILLIAM BURROUGHS S.
IS THIS WILLIAM BURROUGHS S.
THIS WILLIAM IS BURROUGHS S.
WILLIAM THIS IS BURROUGHS S.
IS WILLIAM THIS BURROUGHS S.
WILLIAM IS THIS BURROUGHS S.
THIS IS BURROUGHS WILLIAM S.
IS THIS BURROUGHS WILLIAM S.
THIS BURROUGHS IS WILLIAM S.
BURROUGHS THIS IS WILLIAM S.
IS BURROUGHS THIS WILLIAM S.
BURROUGHS IS THIS WILLIAM S.
THIS WILLIAM BURROUGHS IS S.
WILLIAM THIS BURROUGHS IS S.
THIS BURROUGHS WILLIAM IS S.
BURROUGHS THIS WILLIAM IS S.
WILLIAM BURROUGHS THIS IS S.
BURROUGHS WILLIAM THIS IS S.
IS WILLIAM BURROUGHS THIS S.
WILLIAM IS BURROUGHS THIS S.
IS BURROUGHS WILLIAM THIS S.
BURROUGHS IS WILLIAM THIS S.
WILLIAM BURROUGHS IS THIS S.
BURROUGHS WILLIAM IS THIS S.
THIS IS S. BURROUGHS WILLIAM
IS THIS S. BURROUGHS WILLIAM
THIS S. IS BURROUGHS WILLIAM
S. THIS IS BURROUGHS WILLIAM
IS S. THIS BURROUGHS WILLIAM
S. IS THIS BURROUGHS WILLIAM
THIS IS BURROUGHS S. WILLIAM
IS THIS BURROUGHS S. WILLIAM
THIS BURROUGHS IS S. WILLIAM
BURROUGHS THIS IS S. WILLIAM
IS BURROUGHS THIS S. WILLIAM
BURROUGHS IS THIS S. WILLIAM

WILLIAM S. BURROUGHS THIS IS
S. WILLIAM BURROUGHS THIS IS
WILLIAM BURROUGHS S. THIS IS
WILLIAM IS S. BURROUGHS THIS
IS S. WILLIAM BURROUGHS THIS
S. IS WILLIAM BURROUGHS THIS
WILLIAM S. IS BURROUGHS THIS
IS BURROUGHS S. WILLIAM THIS
BURROUGHS IS S. WILLIAM THIS
S. BURROUGHS IS WILLIAM THIS
THIS IS S. WILLIAM BURROUGHS
IS THIS S. WILLIAM BURROUGHS
THIS S. IS WILLIAM BURROUGHS
THIS IS WILLIAM BURROUGHS S.
THIS IS BURROUGHS WILLIAM S.
IS THIS BURROUGHS WILLIAM S.
THIS BURROUGHS IS WILLIAM S.
BURROUGHS THIS IS WILLIAM S.
IS BURROUGHS THIS WILLIAM S.
THIS IS S. BURROUGHS WILLIAM
IS THIS S. BURROUGHS WILLIAM
THIS S. IS BURROUGHS WILLIAM
S. THIS IS BURROUGHS WILLIAM
IS S. BURROUGHS THIS WILLIAM
S. IS BURROUGHS THIS WILLIAM
IS BURROUGHS S. THIS WILLIAM
BURROUGHS IS S. THIS WILLIAM
S. BURROUGHS IS THIS WILLIAM
THIS WILLIAM BURROUGHS S. IS
WILLIAM THIS BURROUGHS S. IS
THIS BURROUGHS WILLIAM S. IS
BURROUGHS THIS WILLIAM S. IS
BURROUGHS WILLIAM S. THIS IS
S. BURROUGHS WILLIAM THIS IS
BURROUGHS S. WILLIAM THIS IS
IS WILLIAM BURROUGHS S. THIS
WILLIAM IS BURROUGHS S. THIS
IS BURROUGHS WILLIAM S. THIS
BURROUGHS IS WILLIAM S. THIS
WILLIAM BURROUGHS IS S. THIS
BURROUGHS WILLIAM IS S. THIS
S. THIS IS WILLIAM BURROUGHS
IS S. THIS WILLIAM BURROUGHS
S. IS THIS WILLIAM BURROUGHS
THIS WILLIAM S. IS BURROUGHS
WILLIAM THIS S. IS BURROUGHS
BURROUGHS IS THIS WILLIAM S.
THIS WILLIAM BURROUGHS IS S.
WILLIAM THIS BURROUGHS IS S.
THIS BURROUGHS WILLIAM IS S.
BURROUGHS THIS WILLIAM IS S.
WILLIAM BURROUGHS THIS IS S.
BURROUGHS WILLIAM THIS IS S.
THIS BURROUGHS IS S. WILLIAM
BURROUGHS THIS IS S. WILLIAM
IS BURROUGHS THIS S. WILLIAM
BURROUGHS IS THIS S. WILLIAM
THIS WILLIAM S. BURROUGHS IS
WILLIAM THIS S. BURROUGHS IS
THIS S. WILLIAM BURROUGHS IS

THIS S. BURROUGHS IS WILLIAM
S. THIS BURROUGHS IS WILLIAM
THIS BURROUGHS S. IS WILLIAM
BURROUGHS THIS S. IS WILLIAM
S. BURROUGHS THIS IS WILLIAM
BURROUGHS S. THIS IS WILLIAM
IS S. BURROUGHS THIS WILLIAM
S. IS BURROUGHS THIS WILLIAM
IS BURROUGHS S. THIS WILLIAM
BURROUGHS IS S. THIS WILLIAM
S. BURROUGHS IS THIS WILLIAM
BURROUGHS S. IS THIS WILLIAM
THIS WILLIAM S. BURROUGHS IS
WILLIAM THIS S. BURROUGHS IS
THIS S. WILLIAM BURROUGHS IS
S. THIS WILLIAM BURROUGHS IS
WILLIAM S. THIS BURROUGHS IS
S. WILLIAM THIS BURROUGHS IS
THIS WILLIAM BURROUGHS S. IS
WILLIAM THIS BURROUGHS S. IS
THIS BURROUGHS WILLIAM S. IS
BURROUGHS THIS WILLIAM S. IS
WILLIAM BURROUGHS THIS S. IS
BURROUGHS WILLIAM THIS S. IS
THIS S. BURROUGHS WILLIAM IS
S. THIS BURROUGHS WILLIAM IS
THIS BURROUGHS S. WILLIAM IS
BURROUGHS THIS S. WILLIAM IS
S. BURROUGHS THIS WILLIAM IS
BURROUGHS S. THIS WILLIAM IS
WILLIAM S. BURROUGHS THIS IS
S. WILLIAM BURROUGHS THIS IS
WILLIAM BURROUGHS S. THIS IS
BURROUGHS WILLIAM S. THIS IS
S. BURROUGHS WILLIAM THIS IS
BURROUGHS S. WILLIAM THIS IS
IS WILLIAM S. BURROUGHS THIS
WILLIAM IS S. BURROUGHS THIS
IS S. WILLIAM BURROUGHS THIS
S. IS WILLIAM BURROUGHS THIS
WILLIAM S. IS BURROUGHS THIS
S. WILLIAM IS BURROUGHS THIS
IS WILLIAM BURROUGHS S. THIS
WILLIAM IS BURROUGHS S. THIS
IS BURROUGHS WILLIAM S. THIS
BURROUGHS IS WILLIAM S. THIS
WILLIAM BURROUGHS IS S. THIS
BURROUGHS WILLIAM IS S. THIS
IS S. BURROUGHS WILLIAM THIS
S. IS BURROUGHS WILLIAM THIS
IS BURROUGHS S. WILLIAM THIS
BURROUGHS IS S. WILLIAM THIS
S. BURROUGHS IS WILLIAM THIS
BURROUGHS S. IS WILLIAM THIS
WILLIAM S. BURROUGHS IS THIS
S. WILLIAM BURROUGHS IS THIS
WILLIAM BURROUGHS S. IS THIS
BURROUGHS WILLIAM S. IS THIS
S. BURROUGHS WILLIAM IS THIS
BURROUGHS S. WILLIAM IS THIS
S. THIS WILLIAM BURROUGHS IS
WILLIAM S. THIS BURROUGHS IS
S. WILLIAM THIS BURROUGHS IS
IS WILLIAM S. BURROUGHS THIS
S. WILLIAM IS BURROUGHS THIS
IS S. BURROUGHS WILLIAM THIS
S. IS BURROUGHS WILLIAM THIS
BURROUGHS S. IS WILLIAM THIS
THIS S. WILLIAM IS BURROUGHS
S. THIS WILLIAM IS BURROUGHS
WILLIAM S. THIS IS BURROUGHS
S. WILLIAM THIS IS BURROUGHS
IS WILLIAM S. THIS BURROUGHS
IS WILLIAM BURROUGHS THIS S.
WILLIAM IS BURROUGHS THIS S.
IS BURROUGHS WILLIAM THIS S.
BURROUGHS IS WILLIAM THIS S.
WILLIAM BURROUGHS IS THIS S.
BURROUGHS WILLIAM IS THIS S.
IS S. THIS BURROUGHS WILLIAM
THIS S. BURROUGHS IS WILLIAM
S. THIS BURROUGHS IS WILLIAM
THIS BURROUGHS S. IS WILLIAM
BURROUGHS THIS S. IS WILLIAM
BURROUGHS THIS S. WILLIAM IS
S. BURROUGHS THIS WILLIAM IS
BURROUGHS S. THIS WILLIAM IS
WILLIAM S. BURROUGHS IS THIS
S. WILLIAM BURROUGHS IS THIS
WILLIAM BURROUGHS S. IS THIS
S. IS THIS BURROUGHS WILLIAM
THIS IS BURROUGHS S. WILLIAM
IS THIS BURROUGHS S. WILLIAM
S. BURROUGHS THIS IS WILLIAM
BURROUGHS S. THIS IS WILLIAM
BURROUGHS S. IS THIS WILLIAM
WILLIAM BURROUGHS THIS S. IS
BURROUGHS WILLIAM THIS S. IS
THIS S. BURROUGHS WILLIAM IS
S. THIS BURROUGHS WILLIAM IS
THIS BURROUGHS S. WILLIAM IS
BURROUGHS WILLIAM S. IS THIS
WILLIAM IS S. THIS BURROUGHS
IS S. WILLIAM THIS BURROUGHS
S. IS WILLIAM THIS BURROUGHS
WILLIAM S. IS THIS BURROUGHS
S. WILLIAM IS THIS BURROUGHS
IS THIS WILLIAM BURROUGHS S.
THIS WILLIAM IS BURROUGHS S.
WILLIAM THIS IS BURROUGHS S.
IS WILLIAM THIS BURROUGHS S.
WILLIAM IS THIS BURROUGHS S.
S. BURROUGHS WILLIAM IS THIS
BURROUGHS S. WILLIAM IS THIS
THIS IS WILLIAM S. BURROUGHS
IS THIS WILLIAM S. BURROUGHS
THIS WILLIAM IS S. BURROUGHS
WILLIAM THIS IS S. BURROUGHS
IS WILLIAM THIS S. BURROUGHS
WILLIAM IS THIS S. BURROUGHS

I DONT WORK YOU DIG
DONT WORK YOU DIG I
WORK YOU DIG I DONT
YOU DIG I DONT WORK
DIG I DONT WORK YOU

I DONT WORK DIG YOU
DONT WORK DIG YOU I
WORK DIG YOU I DONT
YOU I DONT WORK DIG
DIG YOU I DONT WORK

I DONT YOU DIG WORK
DONT YOU DIG WORK I
WORK I DONT YOU DIG
YOU DIG WORK I DONT
DIG WORK I DONT YOU

I DONT YOU WORK DIG
DONT YOU WORK DIG I
WORK DIG I DONT YOU
YOU WORK DIG I DONT
DIG I DONT YOU WORK

I DONT DIG WORK YOU
DONT DIG WORK YOU I
WORK YOU I DONT DIG
YOU I DONT DIG WORK
DIG WORK YOU I DONT

I DONT DIG YOU WORK
DONT DIG YOU WORK I
WORK I DONT DIG YOU
YOU WORK I DONT DIG
DIG YOU WORK I DONT

Cut-Ups Self-Explained

Writing is fifty years behind painting. I propose to apply the painters' techniques to writing; things as simple and immediate as collage or montage. Cut right through the pages of any book or newsprint . . . lengthwise, for example, and shuffle the columns of text. Put them together at hazard and read the newly constituted message. Do it for yourself. Use any system which suggests itself to you. Take your own words or the words said to be "the very own words" of anyone else living or dead. You'll soon see that words don't belong to anyone. Words have a vitality of their own and you or anybody can make them gush into action.

The permutated poems set the words spinning off on their own; echoing out as the words of a potent phrase are permutated into an expanding ripple of meanings which they did not seem to be capable of when they were struck and then stuck into that phrase.

The poets are supposed to liberate the words—not to chain them in phrases. Who told poets they were supposed to think? Poets are meant to sing and to make words sing. Poets have no words "of their very own." Writers don't own their words. Since when do words belong to anybody. "Your very own words," indeed! And who are you?

CUT THE TEXT INTO THREE COLUMNS:

A	B	C
Writing is fifty y	ears behind painting.	I propose to apply
the painters' techniq	ues to writing; things	as simple and
immediate as collage	or montage. Cut right	through the pages
of any book or newspr	int... lengthwise, for	example, and shuffle
the columns of text.	Put them together at	hazard and read the
newly constituted mes	sage. Do it for yours	elf. Use any system
which suggests itself	to you. Take your ow	n words or the words
said to be "the very	own words" of anyone e	lse living or dead.
You'll soon see that	words don't belong to	anyone. Words have
a vitality of their o	wn and you or anybody	can make them gush
into action.		
The permutated po	ems set the words spin	ning off on their
own; echoing out as t	he words of a potent p	hrase are permutat-
ed into an expanding	ripple of meanings whi	ch they did not seem
to be capable of when	they were struck and	then stuck into that
phrase.		
The poets are sup	posed to liberate the	words—not to chain
them in phrases. Who	told poets they were	supposed to think?
Poets are meant to si	ng and to make words s	ing. Poets have
no words "of their v	ery own." Writers don	't own their words.
Since when do words b	elong to anybody. "Yo	ur very own words,"
indeed ! And who are	you?	

(The letters struck out were those sliced by my scissors. Now, permutate the columns to form the new texts.)

Now I shall read across in the normal way the text ACB, and it says:

Text ACB

Writing is fifty. I propose to apply ears behind painting. The painters' techniques as simple and use to writing; things immediate as collage through the pages or montage. Cut right of any book or newspr example, and shuffle into. . . lengthwise, for the columns of text. Hazard and read them. Put them together are newly constituted meself. Use any system sage. Do it for yours which suggests itself, own words or the words to you. Take your own, said to be "the very else living or dead own words of anyone." You'll soon see that anyone. Words have words don't belong to a vitality of their o can make them gush on and you or anybody into action.

The permutated punning off on their ems set the words spin own; echoing out as phrase are permutate he words of a potent ped into an expanding which they did not seem; ripple of meanings which to be capable of when then stuck into that they were struck and phrase.

The poets are suwords—not to chain posed to liberate the them in phrases. Who supposed to think? Told poets they were Poets are meant to sing. Poets have ng and to make words snow words "of their wit own their words very own." Writers don. Since when do words "ur very own words," belong to anybody. "Yo indeed! And who are you?

Text BAC

Writing is fifty y

ears behind painting, the painters' techniq I propose to apply ues to writing; things immediate as collages as simple and or montage. Cut right of any book or newsprt through the pages int . . . lengthwise, for the columns of text, example, and shuffle Put them together at newly constituted meshazard and read the sage. Do it for yours which suggests itself elf. Use any system to you. Take your o said to be "the very n words or the words own words" of anyone You'll soon see that else living or dead, words don't belong to a vitality of their o anyone. Words have wn and you or anybody into action, can make them gush

The permutated po

ems set the words spin own; echoing out as tning off on their he words of a potent ped into an expanding phrase are permutat-ripple of meanings whito be capable of whench they did not seem they were struck and phrase, then stuck into that

The poets are sup

posed to liberate the them in phrases. Who words—not to chain o told poets they were Poets are meant to si supposed to think? ng and to make words snow words 'of their ving. Poets have ery own." Writers don Since when to words ('t) own their words. belong to anybody. "Yo indeed! And who are ur very own words," you?

Text A + CB

Writing is fifty the painters' technique, immediate as collage of any book or newspr the columns of text. Newly constituted mess which suggests itself said to be the very. You'll soon see that a vitality of their into action.

The permutated poem, echoing out as ted into an expanding to be capable of when phrase.

The poets are sue them in phrases. Poets are meant to sigh now words of their. Since when do words indeed! And who are I propose to apply ears behind painting., as simple as use to writing; things through the pages or montage. Cut right example and shuffle into lengthwise for hazard and read the put them together ourself. Use any system sage. Do it for your words or the words to you. Take your own else living or dead; own words of anyone, anyone. Words have words don't belong to one and you or anybody can make them gush.

Set the words spin phrase are permutate. The words of a potent they did not seem, ripple of meanings then stuck into that they were struck. And words not to chain. Posed to liberate the supposed to think? Told poets they were Poets to make words own their words. Very own. Writer's "very own words" belong to anybody. You and you.

Text B + CA

Ears behind painting; use to writing; things or montage. Cut right into . . . lengthwise. Put them together are sage. Do it for yours to you. Take your own words of anyone. Words don't belong to own and you or anybody aims to set the words spin. The words of a potent ripple of meanings whin they were struck and posed to liberate.

The O told poets they were NG and to make words "very own." Writers don't belong to anybody. You, you?

Writing is fifty. I propose to apply the painters' techniques as simple and immediate as "collage" through the pages of any book or newspr example, and shuffle the columns of text. Hazard and read the newly constituted mesself. Use any system which suggests itself in words or the words said to be "the very else living or dead. You'll soon see that anyone. Words have a vitality of their o can make them gush into action.

The permutated poems running off on their own; echoing out as the phrases are permutated into an expanding which they did not seem capable of when then stuck into that phrase.

The poets are sup words—not to chain them in phrases. Who supposed to think? Poets are meant to si ing. Poets have now words of their own words. Since when do words your very own words, indeed! And who are you?

Sinclair Beiles, William S. Burroughs, Gregory Corso, and Brion Gysin, *Minutes to Go*. Paris: Two Cities, 1960.

CALLING ALL RE ACTIVE AGENTS
I THINK THEREFORE I AM
RUB OUT THE WRITE WORD

Wiliam S. Burroughs and Brion Gysin, *The Exterminator*. San Francisco: Auerhahn Press, 1960.

WHO SENDS THE MAN
KICK THAT HABIT MAN
JUNK IS NO GOOD BABY
CAN MOTHER BE WRONG
SHORT TIME TO GO
IN THE BEGINNING WAS THE WORD
RUB OUT THE WORDS
PROCLAIM PRESENT TIME OVER

Brion Gysin tapes, c. 1960–1963. Digitized 13cm audio tapes. C1400/1–9, British Library.

I AM THAT I AM
NO POETS DONT OWN WORDS
KICK THAT HABIT MAN
JUNK IS NO GOOD BABY
PER MU TA TIONS
IN THE BEGINNING WAS THE WORD
LORD I AM NOT WORTHY
WHO SENDS THE MAN
THIS REALLY SENDS ME MAN
PROCLAIM PRESENT TIME OVER
SHORT TIME TO GO
PLAY IT COOL FOOL
I AM I WHO ARE YOU
THIS COULD BE YOU
WHAT WORDS TO STEAL
DO THEIR WORDS RUB OUT THERE
YOU BELONG TO ME
CALLING ALL REACTIVE AGENTS
LIKE YOU JUST SAID
I LOVE YOU I DO
I GOT THE FEAR
EVERYONE IS AHEAD NOW
BE ON THE BEAT
JUNK IS NO GOOD BABY
KICK THAT HABIT MAN
WHAT ARE YOU THINKING
I DIG YOU MAN
THIS TURNS ME ON
I AM OUT ARE YOU IN
THAT REALLY BUGS ME
WHAT YOU NOT GOT IN THERE
GOT SOME POT
I GOT IT MADE
I AM THE MAN
I AM THE MASTER
THE FUZZ COULD BREAK
LOVE MAKES THE WORLD GO ROUND
BREATHE IN THE WORDS

Brion Gysin, untitled notebook, c. 1964–65. Stuart A. Rose Manuscript, Archives, and Rare Book Library, Emory University.

PLAY ON WORDS
WHO MADE THE WORLD
I AM THAT I AM
IN THE BEGINNING WAS THE WORD
LORD I AM NOT WORTHY
MY MASTER IS THE POET
WHO SENDS THE MAN
THIS REALLY SENDS ME MAN
PROCLAIM PRESENT TIME OVER
SHORT TIME TO GO
PLAY IT COOL FOOL
I AM I WHO ARE YOU
THIS IS JUST THE THING
THIS COULD BE YOU
WHAT WORDS TO STEAL
DO THEIR WORDS RUB OUT THERE
YOU BELONG TO ME
LIKE YOU JUST SAID
I LOVE YOU I DO
I GOT THE FEAR
EVERYONE IS AHEAD NOW
BE ON THE BEAT
JUNK IS NO GOOD BABY
KICK THAT HABIT MAN

WHAT ARE YOU THINKING
I DIG YOU MAN
THIS TURNS ME ON
I AM OUT ARE YOU IN
THAT REALLY BUGS ME
WHAT YOU NOT GOT IN THERE
GOT SOME POT
LOVE MAKES THE WORLD GO ROUND

An Anthology of Concrete Poetry. Edited by Emmett Williams. Something Else Press, 1967.

I AM THAT I AM

Brion Gysin and Ian Sommerville, _Permuted Poems_, c. 1970. Julio Mario Santo Domingo Collection, Houghton Library, Harvard University.

PER MUTED POEMS BRION GUY SIN
IN THE BEGINNING WAS THE WORD
I THINK THEREFORE I AM BRION GYSIN
I AM THAT I AM
THIS IS WILLIAM S. BURROUGHS
JUNK IS NO GOOD BABY
LOVE MAKES THE WORLD GO ROUND
CALLING ALL RE-ACTIVE AGENTS
KICK THAT HABIT MAN
PISTOL POEM

Brion Gysin, _Brion Gysin Let the Mice In_. West Glover, VT: Something Else Press, 1973.

PISTOL POEM
I AM THAT I AM
JUNK IS NO GOOD BABY
KICK THAT HABIT MAN

William S. Burroughs and Brion Gysin, _The Third Mind_. New York: Viking, 1978.

CUT-UPS SELF-EXPLAINED
BREATHE IN THE WORDS
I AM THAT I AM
JUNK IS NO GOOD BABY
KICK THAT HABIT MAN
I THINK THEREFORE I AM
RUB OUT THE WORD
PISTOL POEM
PROCLAIM PRESENT TIME OVER

Brion Gysin, _Songs_. Therwil, Switzerland: Hat Hut Records, 1982.

I DONT WORK YOU DIG

Brion Gysin, _Orgy Boys_. Therwil, Switzerland: Hat Hut Records, 1982.

NO POETS DONT OWN WORDS

Editor's note

This book presents a broad selection of Brion Gysin's permutation poems. Sources include published works, unpublished typescripts, and tape recordings. Occasionally, several different versions of each poem are included to show the development of the work.

A complete chronology has proved difficult to establish, however. Gysin's first permutation poem, "I AM THAT I AM," was written as early as 1958, but the histories of many of the following permutations are complex and unresolved. The reader will note that there are no definitive dates for three major sources cited in this book: the Brion Gysin tapes held at the British Library, the untitled notebook held at Emory University, and the Gysin/Sommerville *Permuted Poems* held at Harvard University (among a few other places).

The tapes in the British Library are thought to have been recorded in the early 1960s. Most were evidently prepared for *The Permutated Poems of Brion Gysin*, a British Broadcasting Company radio program commissioned by Douglas Cleverdon. Gysin worked in the BBC's sound effects studio for three days in 1960,[1] and the resulting edited program aired August 15, 1961, at 10 p.m.[2] Some of these recordings have been released elsewhere, such as in Henri Chopin's *OU* audio magazine (No. 20–21, Sceaux, France: Revue OU, 1962), on *The Brion Gysin Show: Where Is That Word?* (Düsseldorf/Munich: S Press Tonbandverlag, 1975), and on *Recordings 1960–81* (Chicago: Perdition Plastics, 1995). The tapes were also used in Gysin's live performances with Le Domaine Poétique, beginning in the 1960s.

According to the notes accompanying the tapes, tape C1400/2 is a recording of a performance at the ICA in London on March 28, 1963, while the undated C1400/3 was recorded for Sveriges Radio (Swedish Radio). There are no notes for C1400/4; the material on this tape includes incidental background sounds, and may or may not be part of the 1960 studio sessions. C1400/5, which consists of layered and modulated versions of the individual poems, would seem to be a recording of the final, mixed BBC program itself.

Most of the poems on the Gysin tapes correspond to typescripts in the untitled notebook at Emory University. The date range given by Emory is c. 1964–65. These typescripts seem to have been very precisely composed by Gysin, and there are abbreviations and other stylistic features that appear rarely, if at all, in the published work.

I have transcribed several of the tapes that do not seem to have clear or complete corresponding texts. The sound poems present significant transcription challenges, especially since Gysin makes great use of homophony and tone. I have opted not to indicate all possible homophony and have instead chosen words according to the indications of syntax and delivery. I have followed the un-punctuated, uppercase style of the vast majority of the published permutations.

Finally, the Gysin/Somerville *Permuted Poems*, undated and provisionally titled, stands as primary evidence of Ian Sommerville's use of a computer to generate Gysin's poems. This text, of which at least a few copies were made, is a facsimile of the output of a computer line printer. The same printouts appear in *The Third Mind*, where they are introduced as "poems printed on Honeywell Series 200 model 120 computer programmed by Ian Sommerville; 2420 lines of text."[3]

While much commentary has conflated Sommerville's computer-generated permutations with those featured in the BBC program, it's clear from a comparison of the two bodies of work that they are not the same. The *Permuted Poems*—which are, again, the only computer printouts I have been able to locate in Gysin's archives—are structured according to a reverse-lexicographic (revlex) algorithm; the British Library tapes, on the other hand, are more freely composed, and when they do follow a pattern, it's not revlex. Further, the Honeywell Series 200 model 120, the computer credited in *The Third Mind*, was not available until 1965, four years after the BBC program was aired.[4] David Pocknee writes that the earliest published computer algorithm for reverse-lexicographic permutation is R. J. Ord-Smith's BESTLEX ("Generation of Permutations in Lexicographic Order," *Communications of the Association for Computing Machinery* 11, no. 2), published in 1968, which would make Sommerville's earlier use of such an algorithm unlikely.[5]

William S. Burroughs and Gysin composed *The Third Mind* as early as 1965, although the book was likely revised or updated before it was published until 1978. Gysin introduced the computer-generated permutations to Jan Herman, the editor of *Brion Gysin Let the Mice In*, in a letter dated June 10, 1970, and these were first published in 1973. This letter would place the computer printouts somewhere between 1965 and 1970, although, given the publication history of the Ord-Smith algorithm, the date is probably closer to 1970.

1 Brion Gysin, *Brion Gysin Let the Mice In* (West Glover, VT: Something Else Press, 1973), 6.

2 "Schedule - BBC Programme Index," The BBC, accessed December 14, 2021, https://genome.ch.bbc.co.uk/.

3 William S. Burroughs and Brion Gysin, *The Third Mind* (New York: The Viking Press, 1978), 57.

4 *Honeywell Series 200 and 2000* (Delran, NJ: Datapro Research Corporation, 1974), 70C-480-01b. Available at http://www.bitsavers.org/pdf/honeywell/datapro/70C-480-01_7404_Honeywell_200_2000.pdf.

5 David Pocknee, "The Permutated Poems of Brion Gysin," accessed December 14, 2021, http://davidpocknee.ricercata.org/gysin/.

Brion Gysin
Permutations

Edited and designed by Alec Mapes-Frances

DABA
68 Washington Avenue
Brooklyn, NY 11205
dabapress.net

Distributed by
ARTBOOK | D.A.P.
75 Broad Street, Suite 630
New York, NY 10004
www.artbook.com

Printed by die Keure in Belgium

DABA 008
ISBN 978 1 7346817 7 2